ACCOUNTING
in the Soviet Union

ACCOUNTING
in the Soviet Union

EHIEL ASH
and
ROBERT STRITTMATTER

PRAEGER

New York
Westport, Connecticut
London

Library of Congress Cataloging-in-Publication Data

Ash, Ehiel.
    Accounting in the Soviet Union / Ehiel Ash and Robert
Strittmatter.
        p.   cm.
    Includes bibliographical references and index.
    ISBN 0-275-93069-6 (alk. paper)
    1. Accounting—Soviet Union.   2. Business enterprises—Soviet
Union—Accounting.   I. Strittmatter, Robert.   II. Title.
    HF5616.S65A73   1992
    657'.0947—dc20   90-24129

British Library Cataloguing in Publication Data is available.

Library of Congress Catalog Card Number: 90-24129
ISBN: 0-275-93069-6

First published in 1992

Praeger Publishers, One Madison Avenue, New York, NY 10010
An imprint of Greenwood Publishing Group, Inc.

Printed in the United States of America

The paper used in this book complies with the
Permanent Paper Standard issued by the National
Information Standards Organization (Z39.48-1984).

10 9 8 7 6 5 4 3 2 1

Contents

Tables and Figures

Preface

Several books have been published in the Soviet Union on the theory and practice of accounting in the United States. These studies are requirements within the curriculum leading to the conferment of a degree in accounting. They give the Soviet professional an opportunity to select, from an array of accounting methods and techniques, those which might be adopted for use in the USSR. Accounting in the Soviet Union is the first attempt to provide the American accounting professional and others with an analogous opportunity. Our intention is not simply to elucidate the details of accounting procedures in the USSR; rather, it is to concentrate on those that may present the greatest interest to an American readership. The methodology of accounting is examined as a required first step in the evaluation of Soviet enterprise data. The continuing interdependence of accounting, planning, statistics, and the economic policies of the Soviet government is also stressed.

The accounting methodology is the only means in the Soviet Union for collecting, classifying, and summarizing economic information. Economic data may reflect expenditures, the nature of production costs, the productivity of labor, the capacity of an enterprise, the circulation of goods, prices and their formation, or the quality and volume of productive output. Thus, a firm grounding in Soviet accounting theory and practice must precede any attempt to examine statistical data on the Soviet economy, its branches, or individual enterprises.

We sincerely acknowledge Dean Charles O'Donnell of Iona College for his continuing encouragement and support of our efforts, Professors Calvin Engler and Salvatore Palestro of the Accounting Department for their thorough review and pertinent suggestions, and Edward Ackerly and the staff of the Secretarial Services Center for their extensive and exceptional word-processing efforts. We also acknowledge John Emerich, Jr. of Aristide Caratzas for translation of necessary materials.

Introduction

Accounting practice the world over is based upon the double-entry system in which all economic transactions have a clear, logical, and simultaneous influence on the content and correlation of an economic entity's assets and their origins. This does not imply, however, that the practical use of the double-entry system and accounting procedures, as a whole, are free from local sociopolitical influences: governmental structures, forms of property ownership, and national traditions. Each of these factors undoubtedly exercises a strong impact on the theory and practice of accounting in any country. Throughout its history, the Soviet Union and its managerial apparatus have used accounting and economic analysis for management and control of individual enterprises and the entire national economy. Through total control over material, labor, finance, and other resources, Soviet authorities have regulated the economic activity of all enterprises toward predetermined economic and political goals.

In discussing Soviet accounting theory and practice, and sometimes referring to its American counterpart, we are conscious of the fact that each system of accounting has developed within its own peculiar environment, and that every accounting system represents the result of the creative efforts of many individuals and organizations. This is why, reflecting the peculiarities and distinctions of Soviet and American accounting systems, we do not extol the achievements or criticize the deficiencies of either system. We proceed, rather, from the conviction that the reader is sufficiently qualified and equipped to make independent judgments based upon our research. Compared with American accounting systems, the Soviet system has been developed without consideration of the need for income distribution among partners or corporate shareholders. Before recent perestroika reforms, the state, the sole proprietor of all enterprises, appropriated all profits and determined their distribution and use; managers and workers often received distorted information concerning the generation and distribution of profits. In the USSR at this time the use of stocks and bonds is very limited, as are problems associated with market prices and their fluctuation. Nevertheless, with regard to Soviet accounting for plant assets, material and merchandise inventory, manufacturing costs and sales, and several other areas of accounting practice, as well as the theory of accounting and its design, there are many features deserving the attention of American professional accountants.

Specifically unique to Soviet accounting theory and practice is the underlying theoretical influence of the socialist/communist ideology of Karl Marx and Vladimir Lenin. In their early attempts to create a utopian state, the Communist Party and the Soviet government consistently exhorted the population toward achievement of meticulously planned levels of output. Soviet accounting methodology is thus driven toward the twin objectives of economic measurement and economic control. But as the Soviet economy has faltered over the past decades, the dreams of a utopian society have faded. Soviet citizens have developed an awareness of their country's economic failings and the reform efforts of Mikhail Gorbachev have permitted limited economic restructuring. As the process of economic reform gathers momentum, however, the nature, scope, and velocity of changes become more unpredictable. Recent changes have included a reduction in centralized government planning, legitimization of certain free-market activities, and banking reform permitting increased commercial banking activity. We have presented a historical account of the Soviet economic system through the earliest years of perestroika. Readers desiring contemporary knowledge are advised to consult current sources.

In presenting economic data on the Soviet Union, we have utilized recently available official Soviet government sources. However, any analysis and use of this information by readers must be tempered with caution. Data released by the Soviet government in the past was often distorted and manipulated to serve propagandistic purposes. Data currently available may lack accuracy and precision and may be derived from approximations of actual economic conditions and results. The authors' presentation of Soviet accounting theory and practice, and any comparisons with American accounting systems, are based on their personal knowledge of and familiarity with such systems.

I

SOVIET ENTERPRISE MANAGEMENT: THE POLITICAL AND ECONOMIC ENVIRONMENT

Accounting is an economic discipline that cannot be fully appreciated and understood without an understanding of the political and economic environment in which it took root and developed; this is particularly so in a controlled society since economic information is essential for centralized planning and management. Accounting theory and practice prevalent in the Soviet Union are a direct product of the Soviet political and economic system; Soviet culture, national traditions, and the legal system have shaped accounting theory and practice as well. This part will present an outline of the social, economic, and political system of the USSR as a minimum prerequisite for understanding the nature of Soviet accounting.

1

The Social Structure and Policy of the Soviet Union

PROFILE OF THE UNION OF SOVIET SOCIALIST REPUBLICS

The history of the Soviet Union begins in 1917 when Karl Marx's proponent Vladimir Lenin returned to Russia from exile abroad and eventually led the Bolshevik uprising against the provisional government of Aleksandr Kerensky. Lenin promised the peasants land, the workers freedom and equality, the soldiers peace, and one and all the dictatorship of the proletariat with a bright future of abundance and prosperity. With such promises, Lenin, and the Communist Party under his leadership, drew a large part of the population to their cause. Within two or three years they had subdued all opposition and taken absolute control of the country. Until recently, Communist parties have demonstrated an amazing ability to seize and hold power both in Russia and many other countries of the world. Their success has been remarkable considering that Party membership has always consisted of a very small minority of the population.

Individuals always strive toward a better life, creating an ideal society in their imagination. Enticed by the attractive promises the principles of socialism and communism conveyed to them, the people of Russia gave a relatively small group of adventurists the opportunity to do whatever they wanted. Some capitalists and some members of the middle class assisted in the establishment of communism in Russia. Before long, however, many of them realized that they had let loose an evil genie. When power passed into the hands of the communists, the capitalists and bourgeois who had helped them paid dearly for their shortsightedness. Lenin had called them "the temporary fellow travelers of communism" and, as time passed, almost all were killed or sent to prisons and concentration camps to perish. Among the poor, the jobless, the dependent, there are those who dream about socialism and communism as forms of salvation that will rid them of need. Such hopes moved the proletarians as they cooperated with Lenin in establishing Soviet authority in Russia. Although Lenin dispatched the bourgeoisie, liquidating most of its representatives, he soon found that their form of economy was less dispensable.   In 1921 Lenin christened the New Economic Policy (NEP), which, in essence, was a compromise with private entrepreneurs. From 1926 on, however, in another reversal, Lenin's successor, Joseph Stalin, began to wipe out anew the bourgeoisie, which had gradually been reviving under NEP. An intensive period of industrialization, electrification, and collectivization followed.

When the communists began their struggle for power they did not know how they would solve economic problems. They began to experiment in the field of economics after the population had submitted to their authority, and resistance to the communist regime had ceased. The economic promises that the communists so lavishly made before coming into power—abundance of goods, abatement of inflation, full employment, economic equality and security—turned out to be unrealizable dreams, which, from the very first days of the new regime, receded farther and farther into the distance. A joke about this divergence of promise and fact is told in the Soviet Union. Answering the question "What is communism?" a student says to his professor: "Communism is something like the horizon. The closer you get to it, the farther away it is." For the average person, communism, fascism, or any dictatorial system differs from a genuine democracy in a few salient ways: one is deprived of the protection of a trade union, loses all personal liberties, and lacks the right to protest. Since the first days of the Soviet regime people have been expecting that the system would soon topple. But only recently has there been evidence of the degeneration of socialist/communist ideology. Today it is impossible to determine whether the present socialist state corresponds with that envisioned by Marx and Friedrich Engels whose works describe more about the necessity of revolution than the form of society that should develop in its wake.

The Union of Soviet Socialist Republics (USSR) lies within the boundaries of Eastern Europe, Northern Asia, and Central Asia. Its territory covers 22,402,000 square kilometers; 16 percent of the Earth's surface is within Soviet borders. The USSR is endowed with most, if not all, of known natural resources. Pine, fir, larch, birch, and other trees cover 70 percent of the territory of the Soviet Union; this accounts for a third of the world's forest resources. In addition to the water resources of its lakes and rivers, the Soviet Union derives benefit from its access to oceans along its northern and eastern borders. The fauna of the Soviet Union are as rich and varied as its huge territory and many climate zones would suggest; the wealth derived from fur-bearing animals is sizable. The energy resources of the Soviet Union include extensive reserves of hard coal, oil, and gas; hydroelectric power is also abundant. The Soviet Union mines most minerals needed in industry on its own territory; it has one-half of the world's reserves of iron ore. Other plentiful minerals include antimony, asbestos, copper, fluorspar, lead, mercury, mica, tin, uranium, and zinc. A special group of minerals, important in industry, international politics, and international trade, includes diamonds, gold, silver, and platinum. The Soviet Union also possesses huge reserves of these minerals.

The real wealth of the Soviet Union, however, is its people. The population contains many brilliant scientists, outstanding engineers, gifted writers and professors, and talented actors, singers, and dancers. Moreover, Soviet citizens in general attain a relatively high level of education. More than 80 percent of the adult population receives primary or secondary or higher education. The literacy rate of the population is close to 100 percent; almost everyone can read and write in their native language. The population of the Soviet Union is very heterogeneous. Considering only those whose population is 1 million or more, one can count twenty-two ethnic groups. Russians make up the largest group of the total 1989 population of 287 million. The following figures show the general population distribution by occupation: professional and office workers including government employees and party functionaries, 27 percent; industrial and manual workers, 62 percent; and farmers and handicraftsmen, 11 percent. The military strength of the Soviet Union is well known. The country has available at all times not less than 4 million soldiers between the ages of eighteen and twenty-two. An additional 16 million have completed military training and comprise the country's military reserves.

The Soviet Union has fifteen republics, but the multinational structure of the country has recently become shaken due to the many ethnic-based concerns now emerging. Some of the Soviet republics are currently struggling for and will achieve independence from the national Communist Party and separation from the Soviet Union. The estimated population of each republic[1] for 1989 is shown below in thousands:

Russian Soviet Federated Socialist Republic	147,386
Ukrainian Soviet Socialist Republic	51,704
Uzbek Soviet Socialist Republic	19,906
Kazakh Soviet Socialist Republic	6,538
Byelorussian Soviet Socialist Republic	10,200
Azerbaidzhan Soviet Socialist Republic	7,029
Georgian Soviet Socialist Republic	5,449
Tadzhik Soviet Socialist Republic	5,112
Moldavian Soviet Socialist Republic	4,341
Kirghiz Soviet Socialist Republic	4,291
Lithuanian Soviet Socialist Republic	3,690
Turkmen Soviet Socialist Republic	3,534
Armenian Soviet Socialist Republic	3,283
Latvian Soviet Socialist Republic	2,681
Estonian Soviet Socialist Republic	1,573

FROM THE UTOPIA OF SOCIALISM TO THE
UTOPIA OF COMMUNISM

The Union of Soviet Socialist Republics is the first socialist state to be founded on the teachings of Karl Marx, Friedrich Engels, and Vladimir Lenin. For more than seventy years, modified versions of the teachings of these men have provided the ideological foundation of the Soviet Union. Their teachings also have influenced the political systems of countries in Central and Eastern Europe, Asia, South and Central America, and Africa. The Soviet Union has been instrumental in establishing Marxist regimes outside the USSR. Marxist and Leninist social theory affirms that socialism and communism are two phases of one and the same social system. Socialism is the preliminary stage during which two forms of ownership of the means of production exist: ownership by the state and ownership by collective farms and cooperatives. The principles that govern this phase of social evolution are "From each according to his abilities, to each according to his work," and "The one who does not work does not eat." The higher stage of social evolution, communism, preserves only one form of ownership of the means of production and that is ownership by the state. Its governing principle is presumably more humane: "From each according to his abilities, to each according to his needs."

During the Russian Revolution, those who were creating the first socialist state asserted that the results of their efforts would be a new communist society. The Communist Party promised a quick passage from the imperfect socialist phase to the flawless communist phase with all its tantalizing advantages and all its plenty and abundance. Textbooks used in Soviet schools and universities describe a heavenly future:

Under communism all society's springs of wealth will begin to flow profusely. . . . A standard of living immeasurably higher than that of any capitalist country will be maintained. Work will cease to be merely a means of earning money. Human relationships will no longer be calculating and selfish. Society's resources will give to people all that they require for physical and cultural well-being. People will be relieved of onerous cares about their future, about the satisfaction of their material needs. They will thus be free to devote themselves to higher interests. Personal liberty will grow. Political and social rights will develop and increase. There will be complete social equality and freedom. Differences in occupation will not spawn privileges and inequality in ownership or consumption. Reasons to constrain and force people will disappear; voluntary measures will guide society. Relationships of dominance and subordination will be replaced by ones of collaboration and cooperation. The necessity of the State as a political organization will fade away. Methods based on persuasion will replace coercive methods of authority. Self-government will go on in an atmosphere of complete openness. Everyone will be well-informed and active in social matters and self-government. Human reason will develop to the fullest potential of its gigantic might. Man will cultivate his character and sensibility to the fullest. New moral impulses will stir people: solidarity, mutual goodwill, a feeling of deep community with others as members of one human family; unit comradery, fraternity will be the standards of behavior between citizens of one country and between peoples of different societies. . . . And so on and so forth in the same spirit.[2]

The utopia of communism in the Soviet Union came into existence based on the ideas of utopian socialism disseminated over Western Europe. Lenin made the utopia of communism so tantalizing and plausible that people believed in it. Persuaded by promises of future deliverance, people agreed to put up with temporary deprivations and difficulties. After seven decades the tolerated shortcomings, however, have not only failed to disappear, but have become permanently entrenched. For those who grew disappointed and no longer wished to endure the failures of communism, the Soviet government devised an effective apparatus of propaganda and oppression. The existence of such an apparatus explains the Soviet people's long acceptance of a system in which the following ills are rampant: sharp social and economic inequality; extermination and oppression inflicted by the government on its people; a wretched standard of living; the absence of civil rights; slavish dependence on superiors at work; malfeasance, corruption, pillage and hypocrisy; debasement of ethnic identity; and irresponsibility and mismanagement among leadership. Party leaders have long been aware of the fruitlessness of efforts to build a utopian society. However, having come to power and having come to enjoy it, they were hardly inclined to relinquish it because of theoretical errors. The appetite for power became keener in proportion to the degeneration of the utopian idea of communism. The fear of losing power was one of the important motives supporting many of the decisions of Soviet leaders.

THE GORBACHEV ERA

During the years that have passed since Mikhail Gorbachev became general secretary of the Communist Party of the Soviet Union in March 1985, the words *glasnost* (openness) and *perestroika* (restructuring) have become as popular today as Sputnik was in its time. Since openness or publicity may be seen as one of the manifestations of restructuring, we will also assume that restructuring includes the concept of openness in attempting to explain and evaluate what is happening today in the Soviet Union. According to Gorbachev, the architect of restructuring, openness should relate to domestic politics, law, and the economy. Since transformation of the economy is the most complex, difficult, and expensive object of restructuring, Gorbachev and his supporters decided to first restructure politics and legal norms; openness is an integral part of this. Having begun with the loosening of political strictures, Gorbachev aimed to draw the majority of people to his side and win the sympathy of the intelligentsia.

In order to examine the fundamental directions that have been and are being established for future restructuring of Soviet domestic politics, law, and the economy, it is necessary to realize that the basis of any social system is a fully defined ideology which represents the totality of political, legal, moral, artistic, and philosophical views as well as the related economic system. Soviet ideology to the present day remains that of Marxism-Leninism as the Communist Party under Gorbachev's leadership has not renounced any of its basic postulates. There is discussion of their modernization in an attempt to make the ideology more attractive and effective. In his appearances, Gorbachev has repeatedly emphasized a firm intention to preserve and strengthen the socialist system and the Marxist-Leninist ideological basis of that system. This means that restructuring is in essence an attempt at the renewal, recovery, and improvement of socialism. Gorbachev and his supporters have sacrificed the authority and condemned the activities of past leaders (Joseph Stalin, Leonid Brezhnev) to further the rehabilitation of socialism. Perestroika as it relates to ideology, domestic politics, and law may be considered a concession rather than a sincere acknowledgement of the need for democratic reforms. Thus, reforms in the areas of ideology, politics, and law are usually made carefully and deliberately. In the course of relaxation and as a concession to the intelligentsia, the publication of certain works of prohibited authors is now permitted; critical articles are allowed in the press; certain films formerly banned are being released; and some political prisoners and people imprisoned for their religious convictions have been set free. These concessions are in essence designed to attract the intelligentsia who otherwise would be caught up in an epidemic of dissidence. These relaxations are essentially a lessening of control where it had ceased to be effective.

Soviet leaders would like to create a social system in which the economic possibilities of capitalism are combined with the political authority of the Communist Party. But the difficulties of building a new and different economy on a socialist foundation have been demonstrated by the varied reaction to the limited economic reforms that have been implemented. Although these efforts at reform have been viewed favorably in the West, they have generated unfavorable reaction among the Soviet population. The economic adjustment and disruption of reform efforts have produced strikes and increased black market activity. Questions as to the directions and effects of future economic reforms and the possible legitimizing of economic disparity among the people are disturbing to many.[3]

The Soviet Union continues to remain under the authority of the Communist Party, but early in 1990 a plenum of the Central Committee of the Communist Party approved a proposal to end the Party's monopolistic rule. The Constitution of the USSR will be amended to reflect this historic decision. The participation of other groups in political activity will thus be decriminalized and even welcomed and encouraged. This decision by the Party's Central Committee was extremely difficult for the Party leadership but public pressure from Soviet citizens and the realities of similar events in other Eastern Bloc countries made the choice inevitable. At this time the Communist Party still appears strong, but it will probably be forced to yield additional positions and power within the year. It is obvious that neither Mikhail Gorbachev nor his supporters or opponents have developed a clear and coordinated model for solution of the country's economic problems. Developing a model based on capitalist principles and practices will be extremely difficult. Communist rule since 1917 has totally transformed and redirected the economic structure of the country and has, in many respects, created a new genus of Soviet citizens (*Homo soveticus*) who regard any dramatic change in the current economic structure as unthinkable.

2

Characteristic Features of Socialism in the Soviet Union

THE CENTRALIZATION OF POLITICAL ADMINISTRATION AND ECONOMIC MANAGEMENT

Soviet authorities have achieved centralized determination of economic policies and centralized management of the national economy. This centralization is concentrated in the hands of the small group of Communist Party leaders who make up the country's government. The result has been a single-party dictatorship. The significance of membership in the Communist Party of the Soviet Union is not always understood correctly in the West. Although currently decreasing in power and numbers, the Communist Party still has almost 18 million members. It is a mistake to assume that all Party members received unlimited rights and privileges. Certain advantages have usually accompanied Party membership. For example, it was easier for a Party member to become a foreman at work. But non-Party workers also received management positions. Real advantages were enjoyed only at a high level in the Party. Genuinely privileged Party members numbered less than 1 million.

The rulers of the Soviet Union include the members of the Politburo of the Communist Party's Central Committee, the newly formed Presidential Council, and the Supreme Soviet. The Politburo (Political Bureau) presently has twenty-four members including Mikhail Gorbachev, his first assistant Vladimir Ivashko, the first secretaries of the republics, and seven others. The Politburo is headed by the General Secretary of the Central Committee of the Communist Party; at present Mikhail Gorbachev occupies this post. The Presidential Council, consisting of from ten to twelve members, is a permanent body structurally and operationally similar to the president's cabinet in the United States. As the power and influence of the Communist Party has decreased, that of the Presidential Council has increased.

According to the Constitution of the USSR, the highest legislative organ of state authority is the Supreme Soviet, which has about 2 thousand members. The Supreme Soviet is normally convened twice a year when it rubber-stamps recent government decisions, but recently its influence has been increasing.

Voting is by open ballot and, until the era of glasnost, no member had ever voted against a previously prepared resolution. Glasnost has also prompted some members to express their opinions more openly. Between sessions of the Supreme Soviet, a group called the Presidium acts on its behalf. Its members are elected during the semiannual sessions of the Supreme Soviet. Mikhail Gorbachev, elected president of the Supreme Soviet and its Presidium, thus functions as president of the country.

The Council of Ministers is charged with implementing government policies. The Council consists of various government bodies (ministries, committees, organizations) that function at both the national level and republic level. These administrative units handle the affairs of all political and economic branches of the state. Within the Council of Ministers there are several special central organs of administration: the State Planning Committee (Gosplan USSR), the State Committee for Prices, the State Committee for Labor and Salaries, the State Committee for Science and Technology, the State Construction Committee, the Committee for State Security (KGB), and the Central Statistical Administration.

The Council of Ministers of the USSR includes all national-level ministers and the chairman of the council of ministers of each republic. The Council performs the following functions:

1. Management of the national economy, in which capacity it sets pricing policies, regulates the circulation of money and the credit system, sets up and controls the system of labor payment, controls the single system of accounting and statistics, and supervises the management of organizations including manufacturing, trade and service enterprises, and banks and other financial institutions;
2. Planning, in which capacity it develops current and long-range plans, formulates the state budget and monitors the fulfillment of plans and budgets;
3. Management of government property and social order, in which capacity it protects state property, maintains law and order and administers organs of government security;
4. Management of the military, in which capacity it commands the armed forces and manages annual military conscription;
5. Control of foreign policy, in which capacity it oversees diplomatic relations and formulates international trade policy.

Neither a single important economic question nor a significant matter of foreign or domestic policy in the Soviet Union can be resolved without ruling directives from the Presidential Council, Politburo, and, until recently, the Secretariat of the Central Committee of the Communist Party. Such extreme centralization stems from principles formulated by Vladimir Lenin.

STATE OWNERSHIP OF THE MEANS OF PRODUCTION

The economy of the Soviet Union is based on state ownership of the means of production. Such complete and undivided ownership of all means of production has never existed in the history of any society. Socialist ownership in the Soviet Union exists in two forms: state ownership and cooperative ownership (collective farms). Personal ownership by individual citizens is strictly limited: One is permitted to own a one-family house, an automobile, and items such as a television and a refrigerator; all such items are considered personal property. The state alone retains the right to own land and natural resources. Enterprises, collective farms, and other institutions received, for long-term use, the premises they needed to carry on their operations, but these premises never became their property. Very small plots of land have been given to individual citizens, usually for agricultural use, but until recently generation of profits from use of such plots was strictly forbidden.

The economic and political nature of state ownership of the means of production in the Soviet Union is often misunderstood in the West. Some are prone to see in state ownership a form of cooperative ownership and a foundation for well-being and fairness in society. This misconception results from the distortion of reality wrought by Soviet propaganda which represents ownership by the state as ownership by society. The official terminology used to describe state ownership of the means of production does not explain its nature. No single person nor any single group has society's property at its disposal; any attempt at possession is considered a criminal act. According to Soviet law, such an offense would be strictly penalized, with capital punishment not excluded.

Even on collective farms and in enterprises organized on a cooperative basis, where according to their common conception members are assumed to be co-owners, all property actually remains at the disposal of the state. Furthermore, the existence of a form of property considered to be society's is viewed by communist theorists as a transitory phenomenon. Under communism such property, it is supposed, will ultimately belong to the state; that is, it will lose even the external appearance of belonging to society or being in the hands of a cooperative or collective organization. In spite of this doctrine and past practices, limited efforts have been made by Gorbachev to transfer state ownership of the means of production to private enterprises. It is very difficult, however, to attempt to predict the future extent and success of these reforms.

SOVIET PLANNING: ORGANIZED MISMANAGEMENT

The centralized system of planning and accounting in the Soviet Union is essential to the functions of state and party. If one can state that in free-enterprise countries the hidden forces of market supply and demand rule the economy, then one can observe in the Soviet Union that the dominant forces are centralized planning and accounting, which not only determine supply and demand but shape all market relationships. Thanks to the centralization of planning and accounting, the government has not only been able to limit supply, curtailing the production of any goods it selects, but it also can attempt to steer demand in desired directions. Unsatisfied demand in the past caused no complications, for dissatisfaction with economic policy was easily suppressed.

Planning and accounting constitute the mainstay of the Soviet government's system of control over the country's industrial enterprises. Lenin foresaw the use of planning and accounting as instruments of control in socialist and communist economies. Several remarks of Lenin illustrate his foresight:

> Socialism is inconceivable . . . without planned State management, which forces tens of millions of people to adhere strictly to a single norm of productivity and distribution of products. [1]
> Only the social structure that will work according to a large-scale general plan will deserve the name of socialism. [2]
> Accounting and control—that is the main thing needed to set right the first phase of communist society.[3]

Soviet economic planning emphasizes the composition of plans that will enable the economy to develop harmoniously. There are numerous and varied guidelines taken into consideration during the composition of an economic plan: the kinds of products to be produced and their quality, distribution, and sale; the manufacturer's revenues, expenditures, and profitability; the growth of labor productivity and the efficiency of equipment use. Depending on the length of the period for which the plan is intended, some are considered current (for the present year only) and others are regarded as long-range (covering five, ten, fifteen, twenty, or more years). Directives of the Central Committee of the Communist Party are issued to the State Planning Committee of the Council of Ministers before composition of any economic plan. The State Planning Committee bases its plans on these directives.

Official Soviet sources once proudly proclaimed that all plans were composed on a sound scientific basis, and that thousands of scientists and experts developed the plans with the participation of major economic research centers. This was only partly true. Indeed, many people and institutions still actually work on composing economic plans, but the implication that good planning results is misleading. Since planners are not given reliable information they naturally create plans that are unrealizable. An economic plan is usually drawn up through the simple addition of several percentage points to the level of production attained in the previous year. The information with which planners begin has already been distorted; it has been altered to present an embellished picture of the previous year's production. Plans created on the basis of such information cannot be realistic. For planned levels of production for the economy to be achieved, Soviet enterprises must adjust their plans to effect a balance between planned and actual output.   These adjustments continue for almost a year after that for which the plan was intended. In the end, continuously adjusted plan figures correspond with actual figures. The mutual dependence of planning and accounting is revealed in these efforts to adapt the original plan to reality.

The role of central planning as the single means of controlling and managing the Soviet economy has contributed to the economy's many shortcomings.   Some failures that central planning engenders should be mentioned. Since a Soviet enterprise's only interest is fulfilling its economic plan by distributing and selling what the plan dictates, the enterprise often resorts to senseless and wasteful methods of distribution. Thus, cross-hauls are a common occurrence. A train carrying timber from Moscow to Murmansk will pass another train carrying timber from Murmansk to Moscow. A truck hauling furniture from Rostov to Leningrad will pass another truck hauling the same kind of furniture from Leningrad to Rostov. Goods will be distributed without regard for their suitability to the market as long as the enterprise carries out its plan. It is not infrequent that warm felt boots will be sent to be sold in hot Turkmenia, while light sandals will be placed on sale in frigid Siberian cities. Shortly before summer, some stores will receive winter clothing and heavy boots; then at the beginning of winter, they will receive a shipment of summer clothes. Enterprises often receive materials that are unnecessary, and at the same time lack essential materials. Many instances are known of major industrial facilities having been built in areas devoid of the materials and labor needed to run them; when the enterprise finally manages to turn out products there are no consumers for them. In the West it takes the most incompetent businessmen to create such situations. Under his perestroika reforms Gorbachev will seek to limit central planning to only the most important and generalized goals and indices. Efforts will be made to limit the effects of central planning on individual enterprises' internal activities. The Supreme Soviet, however, in late 1989 again approved a centralized five-year plan indicating the government's resistance to movement away from the existing process of planning and economic control.

CENTRALIZED REALLOCATION OF THE NATIONAL INCOME

In both the United States and the Soviet Union the gross national product is regarded as the sum total of material products and services that the society produces in one year through the labor of its workers. All material products are classified according to their natural form and function as either means of production or objects of consumption. Means of production include materials, machines, instruments and other items that will be reused in the production of gross product during the next production cycle. Objects of consumption, on the other hand, are used up. Until recently, the directives of the Central Committee of the Communist Party required the State Planning Committee of the Council of Ministers to plan for expansion in production of the means of production category of products (Group A) to the detriment of the objects of consumption category (Group B). Now, the Party under Gorbachev plans to increase production of the objects of consumption.

On the basis of value, the gross national product can be divided into first, the value of consumer resources, for which compensation must be received and which must be replaced when consumed and, second, newly created value which represents the national income, and can be reallocated (redistributed). Neither individuals nor groups of Soviet citizens have any influence on the composition of the gross national product, the size of the national income, or its reallocation. These functions continue to be the prerogative of the Soviet government and the Communist Party. Some Soviet economists claim that similar situations exist in countries having free-enterprise systems; they assert that in the West no one can influence the formation of the gross national product, the national income, or the redistribution of resources. To rebut such assertions it can be observed that, in a free-enterprise economy, people influence the whole mechanism of supply and demand. Industry produces not what the government wants it to produce, but what people will buy, and people buy not what is thrust upon them by the government, but what they prefer. Investors put their money not into what the government orders them to, but into what provides the highest return. No such process has occurred in the Soviet Union. The State Planning Committee, acting on behalf of the government and the Communist Party, assumed the functions of natural economic forces. Only now has the government recognized the need to consider the influence of market demands on the economy.

The trustworthiness of any statistical data relating to the Soviet gross national product, the national income, and their reallocation must be considered dubious. Data of this nature are generally obtained from official Soviet sources such as the Central Statistical Administration. The 1988 Gross National Product of 1,525 billion rubles may be analyzed by branch of the economy as follows: industry, 912.4; agriculture, 259.7; construction, 165.5; transport and communications, 73.5; trade and other branches, 113.9. The national income, consisting of the gross national product less expenditures subject to compensation, was 630.8 billion rubles for 1988. The Soviet government in 1988 used about 153 billion rubles for accumulation of capital and investments intended primarily for further expansion of the means of production (Group A products). The government directed about 466 billion rubles toward production of objects of consumption (Group B products). It must be remembered that expenditures for maintenance and equipping of the military are within the objects of consumption category. Resources designated for the maintenance of the armed forces are not subject to limitations or cost ceilings. Expenditures for any item of consumption can be reduced as long as ample resources remain for the military.

THE SOCIAL SYSTEM OF THE SOVIET UNION

Marxist-Leninist theory distinguishes five forms of society: primitive communal, slave-owning, feudal, capitalist, and communist. It further asserts that each social system or society has its own distinctive productive forces and relations of production. Productive forces refer to the relationship of people to the objects of production, the means of production, and the products of production. Relations of production describe the social relationships of people in the production process. Communist Party ideologues and those expected to share similar ideas (politicians, economists, sociologists, scientists, and scholars) argued that socialism and communism represent the perfect or highest stage in a society's development. Under communism, demands will be made of people on the basis of their abilities while people will receive dependent on their needs. However strange it may seem, the obvious naivety of the fundamental formula of communism has not repelled or offended people. But dreams of the paradise promised by communist theory have been broken by the harsh economic realities now being faced by the people of the Soviet Union and its neighbors.

Using the societal traits that communist ideologies themselves have distinguished, one may attempt to determine which form of society corresponds to that existing in the Soviet Union. For what one calls the system matters little; what matters are the realities of the system. In the Soviet Union the entirety of political and economic authority has been monopolized by the Communist Party providing it with unlimited control over the objects, means, and products of production and over the workers themselves. From this point of view, the Soviet government thus far possess all the rights and privileges of a slaveholder. The social relations of the people involved in the production process are antagonistic as they are in a slave-owning society. The antagonism between those holding power and the general body of the population is exceptionally strong and growing steadily. The characteristic traits of the Soviet system show its correspondence with that of a slave-owning society: dependence of subordinates on the arbitrary will of bosses; abuse of authority at all levels by those in control; interference of bosses and Party bureaucrats in the private lives of citizens; servility and toadyism of subordinates to those above them in the Soviet hierarchy; a Mafia-like caste system among the Soviet elite who are linked by friendship, family ties, and mutual backing; relative impoverishment of the population; illegal collusion among a large portion of the population in efforts to satisfy their needs for food, clothing, and housing; epidemic suspiciousness, intimidation, bribery, secrecy, and informing on others to the authorities.

Disagreement with authority is increasing within the Soviet Union. The number of citizens who understand and accurately appraise the Soviet system, its ideology, and leadership continues to increase. More have come to view their leaders as oppressors intoxicated with power. Those who help the ruling clique to suppress discontent, enforce obedience, and preserve power in exchange for small privileges are especially hated. Included are those who work for the KGB, the militia, the domestic forces, and special military units. Nevertheless, there remains a portion of the population which is uncertain about the character of their rulers and which continues to trust them.

Any description of the Soviet social system would not be complete without considering the government's requirement for a working population. According to the Soviet constitution everyone in the country has the right to work; but labor conscription of a sort has existed since the founding of the USSR. Not working in the Soviet Union was considered a criminal offense called *parasitism* (tuneiadstvo) which was used as a basis for criminal prosecution. Unable to motivate workers through economic incentives, the Communist Party began to urge citizens to work by using moral and physical pressure. One of socialism's principles, "He who does not work, does not eat," was converted to law. The criminal code of the Russian Soviet Federated Socialist Republic, as well as the criminal codes of the other Soviet republics, provided for penalties for those who do not work, namely, loss of individual rights and confinement in a labor concentration camp for up to two years. Those accused of the crime of not working were characterized as leading anti-Soviet, parasitic lives.[4]

To tighten control over the population the Soviet government administers a system of registration in militia districts. Within twenty-four hours of arrival in a city, every Soviet citizen is obliged to register himself and all members of his family. This is accomplished by submitting personal internal passports for each member of the family. The passports are mandatory documents issued to all citizens at sixteen years of age. When moving, each citizen must have his name removed from the militia files in the city he is leaving and register again in his new place of residence. The militia has the right to deny anyone the right to register thus controlling the privilege of residence. The militia is not obliged to explain denials of residence permission but, without permission to reside in an area, it is impossible to get a job.

It is possible to detect in socialism, as it has taken form in the Soviet Union, the traits of a slaveholding society. Some think that the Soviet system is closer to what Marxists refer to as a feudal system. Still others are inclined to see in the Soviet system a peculiar form of society requiring fresh description. No doubt that in comparison with a slave or feudal society, Soviet socialism has distinctions. Within the Soviet system it is not one person or one family that occupies the role of owner of the means of production and the workers; in the Soviet Union those holding power occupy this role. Another difference can be observed in the level of technology and education. Both are at a primitive level in slave and feudal societies. Soviet socialism has attained a higher technological and educational level. However, the technological and educational levels of the country may be seen as objective factors relating, not to the country's social system, but to the epoch and its concomitant progress.

All of the above having been stated, it must be acknowledged that in recent months gradual changes have developed within the social system of the country. For example, as a result of the Gorbachev reforms, the government has officially agreed to acknowledge the existence of unemployment and to gather data to determine its extent. The government is also considering providing financial assistance to the unemployed. Also, a general liberalization of political administration and population discipline has occurred; people are speaking out and complaining and criticizing the government.

3

The Soviet Economy: An Unadorned and Outspoken View

THE STRUCTURE OF THE ECONOMY BY BRANCH

The economy of the Soviet Union divides distinctly into the following basic branches: industry, agriculture, construction, transport, communications, trade and consumer services, and foreign trade.[1] Industry is the main branch of the Soviet economy. Since the first days of the Soviet regime, more importance has been attached to industry than to any other branch. According to 1988 statistics, there are more than 46,000 industrial enterprises of various character in the Soviet Union. Each maintains its own accounting records and prepares its own financial statements and is thus considered to be economically independent. On the basis of their activity Soviet industrial enterprises may be classified within segments as shown in Table 3.1.

The importance of industrial enterprises predetermines which government body will administer them. Approximately 55 percent of all industrial enterprises in the Soviet Union are run by all-Union ministries and departments; joint Union and Republic or Republic ministries have jurisdiction over 40 percent; the remainder are controlled by local administrative agencies (local soviets and executive committees). Geographical distribution of industrial enterprises in the Soviet Union is uneven. The majority of industrial enterprises are located in the developed European part of the country. All attempts to develop Siberia have not yet produced significant results. Irrational exploitation has almost entirely exhausted energy resources and raw materials in the European part of the Soviet Union. And it is in this part of the country where most of the enterprises needing energy and raw materials are located. At present, Siberia and the Far East provide 90 percent of mined raw materials but obtaining these resources and transporting them to the western part of the country where they are needed entails enormous difficulties and great expense.

Agriculture in the Soviet Union includes two types of enterprises: collective farms and state farms. In 1988, the number of collective farms was 27,300 and workers numbered about 13 million; there were 22,900 state farms

Table 3.1
Classification of Soviet Industrial Enterprises

Segments of Industry	Number of Enterprises	Relative Proportion of Production
Machine-building and metal processing	9,916	21.5%
Foodstuffs	9,338	20.2%
Light industry (textiles and shoes)	8,009	17.3%
Timber, woodworking, pulp and paper	5,401	11.7%
Building materials	3,948	8.5%
Electrical energy	1,424	3.1%
Fuels	1,187	2.6%
Chemical and petrochemical products	1,081	2.3%
Flourgrinding and groats	1,047	2.3%
Ferrous metals, glass, porcelain, pottery and other unclassified[a]	4,827	10.5%

Source: Central Statistical Administration of the USSR, National Economy
of the USSR for 1987 (Moscow: Finance and Statistics, 1988) 81, 87.
[a]Data for this segment were determined by approximate calculation and
should not be considered precise.

with 12 million workers. Collective farms are formally considered enterprises whose property is owned collectively by those working on them. State farms belong entirely to the government. Collective ownership and private ownership in the Soviet Union should not be considered literally. All resources of Soviet industry, agriculture, and other branches of the national economy belong undividably to the state. During the last two decades the number of collective farms has actually been decreasing, while the number of state farms and workers on them has been increasing. In the Soviet Union there are also 6,700 enterprises that are considered joint agricultural enterprises; they are attached to the collective and state farms and serve the various needs of both.

Official sources state that collective and state farms produce 90 percent of agricultural products in the Soviet Union. It is claimed that a mere 10 percent of agricultural products come from the small personal plots that are cultivated independently by collective and state farm workers. The share of Soviet farm products that is grown on these small personal plots and sold primarily on the collective farm markets is actually significantly greater.[2] Agriculture is the weakest link in the Soviet economy. Collectivization of agriculture, the experiment launched by Joseph Stalin in the late 1920s and early 1930s, has cost the Soviet people dearly: its failure manifests itself in constant, and often serious, shortages of foodstuffs. The recent reforms of perestroika, however, have given individual farmers limited freedom to sell their products in free markets.

Construction in the Soviet Union is carried out by two types of organizations: construction contractors and the construction divisions of enterprises. Construction contractors undertake projects on order from those who contract to have the work done. The construction divisions of enterprises work primarily for the enterprises of which they are a part. The total volume of capital investment for 1988 in the Soviet Union is valued at 218.2 billion rubles. This includes the cost of plans and documentation, actual construction costs, and the cost of acquiring domestic and imported equipment. The total volume of capital investment for construction is derived from three sectors: state and cooperative enterprises, approximately 90 percent; cooperative farms, less than 9 percent; and people building their own houses, less than 2 percent.

Capital investment for 1988 can be categorized by economic branch and specific purpose in the following manner: 36 percent was directed toward industry (including military industry); 17 percent toward agriculture; 16 percent for housing construction; 15 percent for trade and consumer services; 12 percent for communications and transport; and 4 percent was directed toward other purposes. Official Soviet statistics do not distinguish military expenditures from civil expenditures. Much is unknown of the enormous capital investment in military industries, for research on military technology, and for construction of buildings and installations having a military use. Also unspecified are the significant expenditures for acquiring military equipment abroad.

Transport in the Soviet Union exists in all known forms. Each method of transport has its own significance and role in the Soviet economy. The huge territory of the Soviet Union and the lack of vehicular roads as well as the low quality of existing roads makes railroad transport the most efficient. Statistics for 1988 divide the total volume of load conveyance (in tons by kilometer) by method of transport as follows: railroad, 46 percent; pipeline (oil and gas), 32 percent; water (sea and river), 15 percent; motor vehicle, 6 percent; and aircraft, 1 percent. The data underscore the extreme importance of railroads in Soviet transport and the insignificant role of motor vehicle and air transport.

Communications represent a highly undeveloped branch of the Soviet economy. Communication enterprises (post offices and telegraph and telephone offices) numbered 92,000 in 1988. In that year in the Soviet Union 9 billion letters were mailed, 50 billion newspapers and magazines were delivered, 250 million parcels were shipped, and 450 million telegrams were sent. The total number of telephones was 40 million but the network of telephone lines is poorly distributed and service is nonexistent in many areas.

Trade and consumer services may be divided according to the two forms of property ownership existing in the Soviet Union; thus, trade may be considered state trade and trade carried out by collective farms and cooperatives. State trade constitutes about 70 percent of goods turnover in the country; the remaining 30 percent is attributable to collective farms and cooperatives. In 1988, there were 716,000 active retail trading enterprises in the Soviet Union. There were 339,000 eating establishments, mostly cafeterias, which were able to accommodate 21 million customers. In 1988, the number of enterprises engaged in consumer services was 303,000; of these about 25 percent made or repaired clothing and shoes on the basis of individual orders; about 13 percent were devoted to radio and television repairs; and almost 30 percent offered such services as saunas, showers, and haircutting. All consumer service enterprises are managed by local soviets and executive committees; all belong to the state.

Foreign Trade in the Soviet Union is the exclusive monopoly of the state. Organizations of the Ministry of Foreign Trade carry out the majority of the country's foreign trade; the international division of the Central Union of Consumer Cooperatives engages in foreign trade on a small scale. The relative proportion of foreign trade with different countries is illustrated by the following official data for 1988: socialist countries of the Soviet Bloc, 66 percent; industrially developed capitalist countries, 23 percent; developing countries, 11 percent. The bulk of Soviet exports consists of productive machinery, transportation equipment, oil, gas, electric power, raw materials and minerals, and arms. The Soviet Union imports complex machinery and transportation equipment, 41 percent of all imports; foodstuffs, 17 percent; consumer goods, 13 percent; and ores, concentrated products and metals, 8 percent. The Soviet Union also imports advanced contemporary technology.

THE STATE OF THE SOVIET CIVIL ECONOMY

Almost all information concerning the state of the Soviet civil economy was secret until recently. Accessible information has often been distorted to present a whitewashed picture of actual economic conditions. If one believed Soviet publications distributed for domestic and foreign consumption, the economy was functioning and developing harmoniously and purposefully. Such a misconception was supported by Soviet propaganda and by the works of Soviet economists. Economists have been obliged to laud the Soviet social system in their pseudo-scientific research. They constantly emphasized the advantages of state ownership of the means of production, the virtues of a planned economy, and the zeal and growing material well-being of Soviet workers. Planning, accounting, and statistics personnel prepared carefully filtered information, which asserted that the supplying of industry, construction, and agriculture was accomplished according to plan, and that plans for production, distribution, and sale were always fulfilled.

In evaluating the actual state of the Soviet economy, one must not confuse the civil and military economies as they are separate and their conditions differ. The state of the civil economy can only be called pitiful.

Contrary to Marxist-Leninist theory, undivided state control of property in the country has not fostered the flourishing of this property, nor has it led to the well-being of the working class. Both the quality and the quantity of products for domestic consumption are decreasing. There are three primary causes for this decline: excessive centralization of economic management, the absence of economic competition, and substandard wages paid to Soviet workers.

Wages that Soviet workers receive for their labors are very low. The average monthly salary in the Soviet Union in 1988 was about 200 rubles, which, using the official exchange rate, is equivalent to 30 dollars. When considering the average salary of a Soviet worker, it must be remembered that the figure includes the salaries of Soviet leaders, army officers, KGB employees, and other privileged workers. By paying its workers so little, the state should have sufficient resources to provide for the basic necessities of the population; this, however, is not the case. The quality of goods produced to meet the needs of the population is low. Even when a sharp need exists, many people prefer not to buy items of clothing, footwear, and linen that have been manufactured by Soviet enterprises. Often the average Soviet worker cannot afford to buy some of the goods that are available.[3] Certain prices are very high relative to wages received: One kilogram of low-quality bologna costs about 3 rubles,[4] a kilogram of coffee costs about 20 rubles, a man's shirt made of synthetic material costs about 30 rubles, while pairs of shoes and boots cost 50 and 80 rubles respectively. A fur coat, 5,000 rubles, or an automobile, 12,000 rubles, requires a huge investment.

Referring to the temporary nature and chance character of particular economic problems, Soviet propaganda persistently exhorted Soviet citizens to be stalwart in enduring these problems for the sake of a brighter future. But people cannot live on ideals alone. The Soviet people strive to maintain normal living conditions under the eternal threat of utter impoverishment. Even in a country where many are informers and where treachery and spiritual slavery are prevalent, people become fighters and cease to fear disproportionate prison sentences and capital punishment. They know that the alternative to taking risks to improve their lot is bleak poverty. The silent resistance of workers to the existing regime is expressed by very low productivity. Workers say to one another confidentially, "They pretend to pay us, and we pretend to work." The basis for planned salary levels set by the government is the minimum income necessary for survival assuming the lowest possible cost of living. The majority of Soviet workers receive approximately the same pay for similar work; the most industrious worker cannot earn more that he is supposed to. The salary fund of an industrial enterprise is established by its economic plan and cannot be exceeded under any circumstances. The cost of the free benefits granted by the government in excess of regular compensation is actually supported by the portions of workers' wages withheld. These amounts are allocated by the state as funding for education and medical service.

The creators of the Soviet system boasted that it was founded on principles that considered basic social equality and the well-being of the people. It has evolved into a system distinguished in the contemporary world by the inequality of its rights and the poorness of its people. Soviet propagandists maintained that the Soviet Union was free of social vices inherent in the West. They exclaimed that there was no unemployment and no uncertainty about the future. They pointed to the existence of free education, free medical care, and the social equality of women. In fact, there is both social and material inequality. Those who perform blue-collar work are at a disadvantage when compared to those in the intelligentsia or management. The children of intellectuals and managers are better off materially and have more opportunities to receive higher education.

Other difficulties result from the exceedingly low level of mechanization and automation in Soviet industry and agriculture. Soviet economists say that 50 million people in the national economy perform manual work. In the most developed countries of the West robots and other automated devices are often used to perform tasks formerly done by hand. In the Soviet Union only insignificant numbers of enterprises use robots. Soviet robots are obsolete, generally unreliable, and often out of use. The use of robots in the Soviet Union is complicated not only by Soviet methods of organizing the manufacturing process, but also by the alienated and heedless attitudes of Soviet workers. The lack of mechanization together with a dramatic decline in the birth rate has now resulted in shortages in the work force.

Labor's rights in the Soviet Union are continually restricted. There is one official union whose existence is permitted by Soviet authorities. Its functions are not the same as those of a union in the West. The Communist leadership in the Politburo and the Central Committee of the Communist Party demand that the union and its enterprise committees induce workers to be more productive and disciplined, inculcate workers with communist principles, and hold the demands of workers to reasonable levels. The union fulfills the role of government overseer and does not function in defense of workers in conflicts with management.

Approximately two-thirds of the circulating or current assets of a Soviet industrial enterprise are used to acquire materials. Since the system of supplying materials works poorly, enterprises accumulate large surpluses to avoid idle periods due to shortages. Consequently, the raw materials inventory of all Soviet industrial enterprises increases faster than the volume of production. There is reason to believe that the future cost of raw materials will be higher, shortages will be more keenly felt, and the labor force will become more inadequate. The primary effects of these conditions will be linked to the production of steel, oil, and other fuels. The slowing of industrial development due to the depletion of natural resources, the lack of automation and mechanization, the insufficiency of the labor force, and the passion for militarization has already resulted in a decline in the rate of development of industrial production from 4 percent annually in the 1970s to 1.5 percent in the 1980s. It is anticipated that this decline will continue.

The Soviet Union has caught up to America in military strength. Often in the past the government has suppressed active dissidence and the independent peace movement within the country and has attempted to tighten labor discipline in its enterprises. The Soviet regime taught its people not to express their thoughts aloud. These shows of strength notwithstanding, the Soviet Union has one signal failure: Its attempts to create a healthy economy and feed its people sufficiently have been futile. The country in essence remains half-developed, lacking roads and telephone lines, and habitually unable to produce food in adequate quantity and goods capable of being competitive in world markets.

THE STATE OF THE SOVIET MILITARY ECONOMY

The military economy, in contrast to the civil economy, has thrived by virtue of the Soviet practice of diverting the best of resources to the military sector. In recent years at least 15 percent of the Soviet work force, approximately 20 million workers, have been employed to meet the demands of the Soviet military forces. Military enterprises never suffer from chronic shortages of materials, equipment, fuel, or labor. The best scientists work in military enterprises. The most advanced technology (including that stolen from the West), the rarest raw materials, and hard foreign currency are all directed into military enterprises. One hundred fifty major industrial enterprises fill military orders in the Soviet Union. In official documents they have been designated as enterprises that issue domestic goods. In addition to the major manufacturers of military products, thousands of enterprises supply the principal producers with military wares such as spare parts and machine assemblies. Thus, in the electronics industry, the majority of integral systems are earmarked for military orders.

There are approximately 900,000 scientists and engineers in the Soviet Union; 500,000 of them, including the best minds of the country and the most talented specialists, work daily in military enterprises. Every improvement, every invention, every discovery is appraised first from the viewpoint of its potential usefulness for military purposes. Soviet military enterprises enjoy another advantage: no importunate pacifists hinder their operation. Thus, in the field of military production, the Soviet Union is beginning to outstrip America. According to calculations of experts, the program of arms manufacturing in the 1980s will cost the Soviet Union about 20 percent of its gross national product. In the United States the share of the GNP directed toward military production is between 5 and 8 percent.

In evaluating the Soviet military economy it should also be remembered that spying produces great benefits for the Soviet Union. To conserve time and resources in negotiating purchases and to preserve its store of scarce and highly valuable convertible currency, the Soviet Union, through its network of spies, steals the newest technology, patents and prototypes of military significance from the United States, Germany, Great Britain, France, Japan, and other advanced countries. The contemporary Soviet spy is a respectable, educated man with a camera, a set of skeleton keys, and a large sum of money for payoffs.

The quality of Soviet military wares is exceptionally high; it is in no way inferior to the quality of military products in advanced western countries. Military enterprises are superbly organized and equipped with the most modern technology and equipment, often bought or stolen abroad; there is none of the mismanagement or indifference to work that characterizes the civil economy. The quality of production in military plants and factories of suppliers is scrupulously controlled by military representatives who oversee production from start to finish. Military representatives are given substantial authority; they are not subordinate to enterprise management.

The sites, products, and consumers of all military enterprises are kept secret with great care. Workers in military enterprises have many privileges and perquisites. They are offered decent housing, land for *dachas* (small vacation homes), and spaces in vacation resorts before other workers. But another side of their work is unenviable since they and their families are under strict KGB surveillance. Revealing information about the products of military enterprises or about their fellow workers is punishable by long prison terms or, in the most serious cases, by execution.

The Soviet government has recently expressed the intention of slowing the high growth rate of military production. It has become more costly not only to produce new, more complicated weaponry but also to use it. The steady increase in the cost of exploiting and modernizing weapons technology has become too burdensome, continually reducing the resources directed into the civil economy. Huge military expenditures compete aggressively with expenditures for consumer goods and health care. Observers interested in Soviet foreign and domestic policies and the country's economy must consider the manner in which the Soviet civil and military economies interact. As the state of the Soviet civil economy has continued to worsen, the foreign policy of the Soviet Union has become less belligerent, softer, and more receptive to negotiations and the conclusion of disarmament treaties.

ATTEMPTS TO FIND ALTERNATIVE SOLUTIONS

In the early 1980s by order of the Communist Party, special groups of economists undertook a lengthy and comprehensive analysis to determine the causes of failures within the Soviet civil economy. In a secret memorandum the experts drew the attention of Party leaders to the following conditions and problems: highly centralized economic decision making and the regulated nature of planning; restraint of market forces; the gap between prices of consumer goods and costs of their manufacture; the centralized system of supplying raw materials and spare parts; centralized regulation of financial incentives for workers; overlapping of management and administration in ministries and agencies; limitation of authority and responsibility of plant managers; domination of administrative management methods over economic methods; development of plans based on unrealistic indicators; and the deliberate distortion of audit findings.

As a result of this analysis of the civil economy, decentralized economic models have been developed in leading economic research institutes of the Soviet Union. Such models assume a limited degree of private enterprise. One alternative being considered by Soviet economists would call for the repudiation of administrative methods based on a high degree of centralization, and the adoption of methods of management allowing for a modicum of private initiative. The recent perestroika reforms under Mikhail Gorbachev are directly related to this alternative. Additional alternatives for improving the civil economy include establishment of joint-venture enterprises in the USSR with Western businesses. Joint ventures have been established with foreign investors from the United States, Germany, and Japan. There is cautious optimism about the long-range success of these arrangements. Those in the hotel and retailing industries have been successful due to the transfer of Western currencies, but other joint ventures operate at a loss or have already failed.

It is worth indicating that a political system that combines authoritarianism and decentralization will not solve all economic problems. Such a hybrid system has been tried in Yugoslavia, which has remained far from prosperity; inflation, recession, and unemployment continue. These problems have increased Yugoslavia's debt and have lowered its standard of living. Communist regimes based on government control and property ownership often create painful political changes when they attempt to develop private property rights and economic initiatives. The transition in Poland, which began with clear and coordinated changes in the political system before moving toward economic adjustment, may in the long run produce less disturbing personal hardships among its citizens. Communist rule in Poland existed for over forty years and limited elements of the former capitalist infrastructure remain. The Soviet Union, among the purest of the communist states for over seventy years, has had virtually no experience with capitalism since the Russian Revolution and the direction, degree, and effects of political change remain uncertain.

4

A Socialist Industrial Enterprise

ENTERPRISE STRUCTURE AND MANAGEMENT

Under a socialist system an industrial enterprise is a state organization. It has at its disposal the material, labor, and financial resources needed to carry out its economic activity which is based on a state plan and is performed under the management of a higher state agency. The enterprise is considered the basic unit of Soviet industry. Each enterprise has property in the form of plant assets and circulating (current) assets granted to it by the state. The enterprise has an independent balance sheet and is considered an existing legal entity with a right to function as a person in legal matters. It can enter into relationships with suppliers, contractors, and cooperating enterprises. An enterprise is created by resolution of a higher state agency acting in accordance with the laws of the Soviet Union or an individual republic. The enterprise functions on the basis of a charter granted by its creating agency. The charter indicates the enterprise's name and location, the name of the agency to which the enterprise is subordinate, and the purpose or nature of the enterprise's activity.

Enterprises within each segment of industry have special features or characteristics. Enterprises may be classified by:

1. Size based on the cost of its plant assets, the number of machines utilized, and the number of workers employed; enterprises are classified as large, medium, or small;
2. Designation or purpose of product manufactured; enterprises manufacture either means of production or consumer goods;
3. Quantity of product manufactured; enterprises may employ mass production, limited-edition (serial) production with a limit for the quantity of product manufactured, or single-unit output of a custom product;
4. Technical level of operation; enterprises are automated,

completely mechanized, partially mechanized, or completely
manual.

In the enterprise, production proceeds through the delegation of certain
functions to various departments or divisions; every enterprise has production
departments and auxiliary (service) departments. The production departments
are the fundamental subdivision of the enterprise. Each is administered
individually by a departmental manager. Each production department handles
a specific task: molding, machining, processing, mixing, assembling, testing.
Auxiliary departments provide the production departments with the supplies
and services necessary for normal functioning: energy, tools, model-casting,
maintenance, and repair. Other auxiliary departments are responsible for
reprocessing spoilage and scrap, packaging, storage, and transportation.
Enterprise management is divided into two groups: line managers and
managers of functional services. Line managers are the managers of the
production departments. Managers of functional services are located within the
planning department, the labor and salary department, and various technical
departments. These departments perform tasks in preparation for production
and make recommendations to line managers during the production process.
A director appointed by the government heads every industrial
enterprise. The state entrusts him with the work of the enterprise. The
director has four assistants. The first assistant to the director (chief engineer)
is responsible for the assimilation of new products, the improvement of
products already being produced, and the introduction of new production
methods and technology; he also acts for the director when he is absent. The
assistant to the director for production is in charge of dispatching the plans that
the enterprise must fulfill; he develops and directs the production processes
required to meet the demands of current operational plans. The assistant to
the director for supply, transfer, and sales manages the procurement of
materials and supplies for production and the sale of the enterprise's products
and services. The assistant to the director for economics (chief economist)
directs all economic activity within the enterprise as well as all economic
service offices; this position is frequently staffed by an accountant.
Enterprise management includes several specialized departments. The
planning department organizes the development of current and long-range
operational plans and participates with line managers in directing activities
having an immediate effect on the current plan. The labor and salary
department monitors the allocation of salaries and the fulfillment of worker
output norms. The technical service departments are responsible for the
preparations for production including the introduction of new products and
automated manufacturing operations. Additional departments with important
functions include personnel, technical control, and accounting. The personnel
department provides the enterprise with its staff and organizes the work of
educational institutions and training facilities within the enterprise. The

technical control department controls the quality of the enterprise's products as well as the quality of all materials and supplies purchased. The accounting department is responsible for keeping accounts for the enterprise's transactions and its monetary and material resources. It also monitors the legality of financial transactions and provides management with financial information about the enterprise's activities.

Until recently within each Soviet enterprise a very special and important role was given to the secretary of the Communist Party organization. The secretary (leader) was elected after being recommended by the regional committee of the Communist Party. In the most important enterprises the recommendation was generated by the Central Committee of the Communist Party itself. The secretary of the Communist Party organization had significant influence in the management of the Soviet enterprise. He participated in the consideration of, and gave final approval to, all important decisions. He was responsible for the ideology and political consciousness of the workers, for carrying out the directives of the Central Committee of the Communist Party, and for organizing ideological meetings and demonstrations. The secretary of the Communist Party organization also controlled the activity of the professional trade union in the enterprise. Ultimately the most important task of enterprise Party organizations, trade unions, and management is the fulfillment of the enterprise's annual technical-industrial-financial plan.

ENTERPRISE TECHNICAL-INDUSTRIAL-FINANCIAL PLANS

Plans for the national economy of the Soviet Union are the basis for all current and long-range operational plans of individual enterprises. An enterprise's operational plan is based on assigned guidelines for its economic activity received from ministries and higher government agencies. The guidelines are broad in scope and form the basis of enterprise plans for the following: the goods to be produced and sold, the acquisition of materials and supplies, enterprise profitability, salary payments and capital investment, transactions with the state budget, and product and process innovation. The overall annual plan of an enterprise is called its *technical-industrial-financial plan* (Tekhpromfinplan). This plan describes the enterprise's productive, technical, and financial activity. The plan has the following subdivisions:

1. A summary of planning guidelines that has been approved by a higher government authority and has been examined and approved by the enterprise;
2. A plan for production, distribution, and sales including the volume of products to be produced, an indication of their quality,[1] an itemized in-kind inventory list, and an export summary;

3. A capital construction plan indicating the overall volume of
   capital investment, the sources of financing for capital projects,
   the enterprise's ability to convert financing into operating
   plant assets and productive capacity, and the return it
   expects for capital investments;
4. A labor and salaries plan indicating personnel needs, salary
   funds, basic pay scales, expected productivity increases,
   and relationships between labor productivity and salaries;
5. A materials and supplies plan indicating the volume of
   deliveries of raw materials, supplies, and equipment, the
   overall material needs of the enterprise, the expected use of
   resources within the factory, and projected efficiencies in the
   exploitation of these resources;
6. A revenue, expenditures, and profitability plan disclosing total
   costs budgeted for the enterprise, costs of producing individual
   products, expected reductions in manufacturing costs in
   absolute and relative amounts, the total contribution margin,
   and the tendency of enterprise income;[2]
7. A financial plan describing the circulating assets of the
   enterprise, the sources for providing required additional assets,
   and the volume of capital construction with indication of the
   sources for its financing.

The reputation of the leadership of government agencies responsible for
Soviet enterprises and the reputation of the Party leadership in regional
committees and trade union organizations depend on each enterprise's
fulfillment of its plan goals. Enterprise efforts will then be rewarded with
thanks and bonuses. If an enterprise falls short of plan goals all officials and
managers connected with the enterprise lose their privileges and bonuses.
Since so much is at stake for the enterprise everything possible is done to fulfill
the plan or surpass its goals: Enterprises operate on holidays, workers put in
extra hours, product output is hastened at the cost of quality, and materials in
short supply are replaced by those of lower quality and reliability.

There exist, however, other methods of achieving plan goals that do not
demand such exertions and do not put such intense pressure on the enterprise.
They allow the enterprise to give the semblance of good performance thus
preserving authority, privileges, and bonuses. The first alternative method of
achieving plan goals is to ensure development of a plan whose goals have been
arbitrarily lowered. The plan must be perceived as demanding the enterprise's
most intense efforts. To obtain approval of the plan, the director of the
enterprise, its Communist Party leader, and its economists utilize the most
intense degree of persuasion when exploiting their business contacts with
officials at the responsible state agency. The fulfillment of a plan thus obtained
will be easy and rewards will be received without much effort.

The second alternative method of fulfilling plan goals requires that information about the enterprise's production levels presented for audit be falsified to show better performance than that actually achieved. Artful accountants, assisted by enterprise managers and economists, work intensely at the end of the accounting period to favorably adjust enterprise financial statements and other auditable information. Several of their ploys should be mentioned: Products not yet completed are recorded as finished and ready for shipment, finished products in warehouses are described as distributed and sold, products falling below standards for distribution can be described as suitable and of good quality. Thus, enterprises have recourse to numerous means of conveying the impression that they have fulfilled their plan. Failures are almost never reported since sanctions for such negligence can be very severe.

The financial statements and reports of individual enterprises will be consolidated several times at different levels by responsible government agencies. Additional consolidation occurs within the statements of ministries and higher government agencies with final consolidation into the All-Union Report that applies to the country as a whole. The Central Statistical Administration of the Council of Ministers, having received the country's annual statement will then, with approval of the State Planning Committee and the Central Committee of the Communist Party, make its own significant modifications in view of higher political considerations. The objective has often been to present the Soviet economy with its best face forward. Many economic indicators will be misclassified or deliberately distorted if they have direct or indirect links to military production or consumption; until recently data concerning the general shortcomings and specific weaknesses of the Soviet civil economy have been carefully hidden.

5

Finance, Money, and Prices
in the Soviet Union

THE STATE BUDGET

The operation of the financial system of the Soviet Union is based on the State Budget, which includes the budgets for all fifteen Soviet republics and local budgets. The preparation, development, and approval of the budget is conducted by the Budget Committee of the Supreme Soviet of the USSR, which receives leading directions from the Central Committee of the Communist Party. The Party uses the budget to further its efforts toward achievement of its political and economic goals. In practice the State Planning Committee and the staff of the Ministry of Finance of the Council of Ministers do the work needed to prepare the budget. As in any other country, the budget of the USSR consists of a part for revenues and a part for expenditures. Prior to glasnost the official budget of the Soviet Union consisted of deliberately skewed data to present a revenue surplus. The State Budget of the USSR for 1988[1] indicated total revenues of 469 billion rubles and total expenditures of 459.5 billion rubles which provided a surplus in excess of 9 billion rubles. Huge accumulated deficits are now recognized with amounts expected to be greater than 100 billion rubles.

Most items in the State Budget are so broadly summarized that it is impossible to evaluate the nature of the actual revenues and expenditures. Some military expenditures are carefully allocated among civil expenditures. An analysis of the 1988 official budget provides the following breakdown: 52.8 percent of the country's expenditures is devoted to development of the national economy, 32.9 percent is directed toward social and scientific programs, while only 4.3 percent is used for military purposes. But the real allocation of the national wealth is different. A large share of expenditures for development of the national economy is used for financing military enterprises and a large share of those for social and scientific programs is spent on education and training of military personnel and on scientific research having a military purpose. Consequently, Western experts and former Soviet economists living in the West believe that expenditures for the military in the USSR amount to at least 20 percent of the national economy; this amount has not decreased under Mikhail Gorbachev's leadership.

BANKING AND OTHER FINANCIAL ACTIVITIES

Banks in the Soviet Union are state institutions. They are the only credit institutions in the country and they carry out all financial operations and monetary transactions. Banking has been highly centralized and is concentrated within five systems: the State Bank of the USSR, the Construction Bank of the USSR, the Foreign Trade and Economic Affairs Bank of the USSR, the Housing and Municipal Services Bank of the USSR, and the Savings Bank of the USSR. Each banking system has a network of offices throughout the country. The State Bank of the USSR is the largest and is responsible for the following diverse functions: implementing the State Budget, issuing paper money and coins into circulation, collecting and accumulating free-money resources, providing short-term operating credit and long-term credit for small capital investments for state enterprises and organizations, accounting for payments between enterprises, handling cash transactions for enterprises, and controlling the financial position and solvency of all enterprises.

The Construction Bank of the USSR finances and grants credit for capital investments in buildings and power and transport facilities; it also handles certain functions of the State Bank of the USSR for construction organizations that it services. The Foreign Trade and Economic Affairs Bank of the USSR organizes and services international accounts that arise from the activities of the Ministry of Foreign Trade and its offices; in addition, it carries out some of the functions of the State Bank of the USSR for institutions that engage in foreign trade. The Housing and Municipal Services Bank of the USSR performs all monetary transactions relating to housing and social service activities. Special savings banks controlled by the Ministry of Finance can be found in every region and almost every populated area. They collect and pay interest on the savings deposits of individuals.

Most payments between enterprises in the Soviet Union do not involve cash. Noncash payments are made by transfer of appropriate amounts from the account of the paying enterprise to the account of the receiving enterprise. Noncash payments may also be recognized by adjusting the accounts of enterprises having mutual obligations to reflect new transactions. Cash payments are used for salaries, pension and benefit payments, and student stipends. Thus, cash circulates mainly in the sphere of personal consumption. The monetary unit in the Soviet Union is the ruble, consisting of 100 copecks and arbitrarily valued by the Soviet government at about $1.75. The actual value of the Soviet ruble in the United States is about $0.05. The ruble circulates only within the Soviet Union as a domestic currency; it is not used in foreign trade. The future status and value of the ruble, however, may be changed as a result of recent proposals for economic reform.

Soviet enterprises acquire assets from four primary sources: financing from the state, short and long-term credit from banks, the profitable operation of the enterprise itself, and subsidies from the state. Financing is an allotment of resources from the State Equity Fund or the State Budget to the enterprise for its permanent use. Though financing is considered a permanent source of assets, the state may adjust the amount at any time; the state may withdraw financing completely if deemed necessary to liquidate the enterprise. Credit is the allotment of resources to an enterprise for temporary needs.[2] Loans are granted for a definite, limited period of time on the basis of the financial security of the borrower. The profitable operation of an enterprise provides resources through the withholding from the state of a portion of the profit earned on the sale of products and services, and through the deduction of depreciation on plant assets. Some enterprises operating at a loss have the right to receive state subsidies. These enterprises do not have access to normal sources of revenue or are unable to earn sufficient revenues to generate a profit. Military enterprises normally operate at a loss and are likely to be subsidized, but information concerning subsidies is kept secret.

THE SELF-SUPPORT PRINCIPLE

The principle of self-support is the keystone of the financial activity of most Soviet enterprises. Soviet financial experts borrowed the principle from the West and imparted to it socialist content and form. Self-support requires offsetting operating costs of an enterprise with revenues from its activity; the enterprise should be profitable, it should always operate in the black. The essence of this requirement can be variously summarized as follows: commensurability in money value of the enterprise's expenses and revenues; earning a profit not less than that projected by the enterprise's annual plan; achieving a production level that results not only in self-support but also in profitability. Stated simply, every self-supporting enterprise should generate an income sufficient not only to offset the costs of operation but to earn a profit. Each self-supporting enterprise is considered economically independent and separate from others within the framework of state-approved plans. Enterprise management budgets and controls enterprise economic activity and directs the workers toward fulfillment of the enterprise's specific goals and ultimately the state's economic plan. Each enterprise has its own cash account in the State Bank with these monetary resources at its disposal. Within the limits of legislative regulations, the bank is empowered to control the enterprise's activity and to enforce these regulations. Each enterprise controls the assets entrusted to it by the government. Each enterprise is responsible for its own accounting records and reports, including its financial statements.

The ruble is the monetary measurement standard for the enterprise's economic activity and financial results. The enterprise itself, as well as the state agencies to which it is responsible, controls the activity of the enterprise using the ruble as the measurement device. This means that the amount of rubles expended by the enterprise must be matched by the amount earned. This also means that the results of the enterprise's economic activity, its profits or losses, must be measured and expressed in rubles. Required payments to the state must be made punctually. In all transactions involving mutual payments among enterprises, each must act responsibly, observing the terms of any agreements and meeting all resulting obligations.

Material incentives are not entirely lacking in the Soviet economic system. The state attempts to motivate enterprises, labor collectives, and the workers themselves by making them feel that they have something to gain from the positive results of an enterprise's activity. Thus, the state provides for the formation of special funds from which bonuses for the enterprise and its workers can be drawn. This is to encourage the enterprise and its workers to complete successfully the tasks assigned. While material incentives tend to motivate the enterprise to operate effectively, material penalties deter it from ineffective operation. The enterprise, its managers, and workers are theoretically responsible to the state and to the enterprise's suppliers and customers for poor results. If performance is below par, however, it is the state that penalizes the enterprise by imposing fines and reducing bonus funds.

PRICES AND THE ESTABLISHMENT OF PRICES

Prices function as an instrument for implementing government policy within the national economy of the Soviet Union. Acting through the State Committee for Prices of the Council of Ministers, the Soviet government shapes wholesale price trends for most industrial products used by enterprises within individual segments of industry. The government also sets tariffs on the conveyance of goods and controls the wholesale and retail prices of the most important goods and services consumed by the population. A limited number of wholesale and retail prices for products manufactured and sold within Soviet republics are controlled locally.

The cost factor, the outlay of resources required to create a product, has been the theoretical foundation of pricing in the Soviet Union. The influence of supply and demand on the distribution and sale of the manufactured product receives only secondary consideration. This subordination of supply and demand contrasts with the role they play in free-enterprise economies where prices are dependent on what consumers want and what is available. If demand for a product is great and supply is not, the price of the product will rise and the entrepreneur will earn a large profit; if demand for the product is low and there are many competitors producing the product the entrepreneur will be forced to set a lower price and be satisfied with a smaller profit. In the latter situation the entrepreneur will devote much of his attention to finding a product that will be more in demand and suffer less from competitive pressures. Ignoring these mechanisms of price formation, the Soviet government set prices by emphasizing the cost of creating a product. Here Marxist and Leninist theorists committed one of their worst economic errors. Frequently, however, the political considerations affecting pricing policy were often more influential than the cost factor.

The system of price-setting in the Soviet Union embraces both wholesale and retail prices and government purchasing prices. Government purchasing prices are those at which the state buys agricultural products from collective and state farms. These prices are very low, but collective and state farms are obligated to sell their products to the government at these prices. This is a significant factor in explaining the habitually low level of farm production. The Council of Ministers of the USSR is directly responsible for setting these prices; the cost factor is not a consideration.

Enterprises' wholesale prices are equivalent to a product's cost to the enterprise plus the enterprise's planned profit. The product's cost is the planned average manufacturing cost for the product in the enterprise's specific segment of industry, not the enterprise's own manufacturing cost. Industry wholesale prices are the prices established for sales among enterprises. They consist of enterprises' wholesale prices, sales tax, and corrections mandated by the state. Sales taxes are periodically withdrawn by the state as budget revenue. By manipulating industry and enterprise wholesale prices the state helps certain industries to prosper while it slows the development of others. These manipulations were often based on political considerations.

Retail prices are the prices at which goods and services are sold to the public. As with wholesale prices the state is frequently motivated by political considerations in its determination of retail prices. The interrelationship of supply and demand and the cost factor are given secondary consideration. Certain products selling at retail are given special consideration in the Soviet Union. For products regarded as necessities (bread, milk, butter, meat, poultry) the state sets prices that are below the price level of these goods on the world market. The prices set on such goods often do not cover the costs to the enterprises producing them with the result that the state must support these enterprises with subsidies. The state's pricing policy on these products results from its recognition that the average Soviet worker, earning about 200 to 250 rubles a month, would be unable to afford basic food products unless their prices were artificially reduced. Raising prices on these products would incite the overwhelming majority of the Soviet people against the Party and the government. Increases in food prices provoked riots in Poland and the potential for such uprisings now exists even within the Soviet Union itself. So the government continues the policy of deflating prices on necessary foods, one unusual result being it has become less expensive to feed animals with certain products intended for human consumption than with fodder. Setting retail prices for other consumer goods is much less difficult for Soviet authorities. Luxury goods are not required for subsistence; their buyers are few and their dissatisfaction is easily ignored. The prices set by the government on such goods are very high.

DOES INFLATION EXIST IN THE SOVIET UNION?

Ideally, the sum of paper money in circulation should strictly correspond with the sum of the prices of all goods in circulation and the value of all services rendered to the people. The specific formula for calculating the sum of monies that should be in circulation at any given time is more complicated, but in this explanation the above will be sufficient to illustrate the primary factors. Violation of the correspondence between the sum of money in circulation and the sum of prices of goods and services causes inflation or deflation. Inflation is the more typical phenomenon; it is reflected by the reduction of the value of money in circulation. Inflation occurs when additional money is issued while the quantity of goods and services in circulation remains the same. A second set of conditions leading to the economic phenomenon of inflation is characterized by a similar imbalance: the mass of goods and services decreases while the sum of money in circulation remains the same. Deflation is the opposite phenomenon, it is relatively rare and has not occurred in the Soviet Union.

The ideologies of Marxism and Leninism assert that inflation is a phenomenon peculiar to capitalist economies. The socialist economy, it is claimed, is free of such an affliction owing to central planning and control of retail prices; the Soviet government supposedly maintains the ideal correspondence between the sum of money and the quantity of goods and services in circulation. Do the leaders of the Soviet State have sufficient grounds for such optimism? It is clear that they do not. In the Soviet Union both causes of inflation exist at the same time owing to increases in the mass of money in circulation and reductions in the mass of goods and services available.

Throughout Soviet history the Communist Party and the Soviet government have continually acted to conceal inflation of retail prices. This activity has taken many forms: the names of goods were changed; different grades were established to give the impression of qualitative change; external appearances, weights, and sizes were altered. As it surreptitiously raised prices on many goods whose demand had increased, the Soviet government publicized, with great fanfare, the lowering of prices on items such as buttons, needles, and thread. The news would be hailed on the front pages of newspapers and on the covers of magazines. On radio and television authoritative economists, speaking on behalf of the government, dutifully calculated that, as a result of price reductions on buttons, needles, and thread, the people of the country would, over a ten year period, save billions of rubles on their sewing expenses.   Enthusiasts appeared to acclaim the Party's achievement and to thank the government for their concern for the welfare of the people.   Experts outside the Soviet Union consider that, in spite of the efforts of the Soviet government, inflation has been at least 5 percent per year. The economic reforms of perestroika and now legal but limited private enterprise activity have recently contributed to much greater inflation.

Perhaps American readers will be amazed at the efforts of Soviet authorities to conceal an inflation rate of 5 percent a year since Americans are quite familiar with an inflationary economy.   However, it should be borne in mind that price increases in the United States are often accompanied by the demands of labor for salary increases to meet or exceed the price increases. The single trade union in the Soviet Union would hardly come forth to demand a cost-of-living raise for Soviet workers; instead, the union would find reason to sing the praises of the Party and the government. American workers have another advantage over their Soviet counterparts: they have a range of similar products from which they may choose the more expensive or the less expensive. Few such choices exist for Soviet workers.

The Soviet ruble is not a convertible currency.[3]   It cannot be used abroad, nor can it be exchanged for other currencies.   The ruble is backed by the mass of goods that the country produces and puts into circulation.   Since goods have been chronically scarce throughout the seventy-year history of the Soviet Union, the amount of money in circulation has always been significantly greater than the amount of goods available.   As a result, large monetary reserves have accumulated among certain segments of the population.   This surfeit of money in circulation constitutes nothing other than inflation.   On the other hand, the Soviet people do not have confidence in the ruble.   They continually search for spending opportunities which often lead to their buying items that are not needed, sometimes paying 10 to 20 times their worth.   Many buy jewelry and other valuables which can be hidden from the authorities. Recently Soviet citizens have been allowed to possess and open bank accounts in foreign currency; these funds can now be spent in special stores selling the best domestic and foreign goods.

6

The Alternative (Underground) Economy

CONDITIONS FOR THE EMERGENCE AND EXISTENCE
OF AN ALTERNATIVE ECONOMY

The Soviet economic system creates conditions leading to the emergence of crimes peculiar to socialism, that is, economic crimes arising from the deficiencies of the economic system itself. The root of the matter is the Soviet system's failure to rid workers of poverty; additionally, the system has added personal debasement to poverty and, until recently, has forced the population to remain silent about its dissatisfaction. Classified studies performed by Soviet economists concluded that the minimum income necessary to satisfy the subsistence requirements of a family of four is at least 850 rubles per month. How then can millions of families subsist when the average monthly income of two working parents is less than 300 to 400 rubles?

The Soviet economic system with its deficiencies and inequities has forced many within the country to resort to illegal forms of economic activity for survival. They fill private orders for goods that they themselves manufacture, they buy scarce goods and resell them at a profit, they illegally raise domestic animals, and they give and take bribes. Those who work in stores and restaurants steal materials, foodstuffs, and finished products from the state. The more ambitious open underground enterprises where they produce goods most in demand, selling them through state trading outlets. All of these activities are considered serious crimes. Highly respectable Soviet citizens are often enmeshed in this illegal economic activity. One can find violators of economic laws among enterprise directors, Communist Party organizers, militia officers, judicial employees, and professors. From the standpoint of Soviet law, at least 70 percent of the population commits at least one economic crime per day. Criminal economic activity has engendered an alternative or underground economy that exists side by side with the official economy. The alternative economy attracts large numbers of people who conspire with one another to find means to supplement their authorized salaries. The understanding that such endeavors are necessary unites people;

they become accomplices and partners in searching for methods to break the state's hold on property and wealth. Participating in the underground economy is dangerous, but it is considered necessary for survival.

The significance of illegal economic activity is briefly and precisely described by Roman Redlikh in his book about Soviet society.

> The spontaneous development of private enterprises, together with the corruption in the Party and in the fulfillment of state economic plans, undoubtedly plays not only an economic, but also a political role in Soviet society. We have here actually a difficult-to-catch organization within an organization which is functioning without the ruling and leading Party nucleus. Its development, however, only in theoretically imaginable limits, may become dangerous for the existing dictatorship, and this is why the occasional measures undertaken against it by the government have a more psychological than an economic or political character.[1]

TYPES OF UNDERGROUND ECONOMIC ACTIVITY

Economic crimes account for at least 25 percent of all criminal activity within the Soviet Union. Most economic crimes are directed against state property or the property of collectives and cooperatives. It should be made clear that the underground economy frequently lives parasitically off the body of the official economy. The underground economy often co-opts the resources of state enterprises; however, state enterprises benefit from existence of the underground economy. It is sometimes impossible for a state enterprise to function without utilizing the materials and supplies available from the underground economy. In essence, all Soviet citizens are involved in the alternative economy to a greater or lesser extent. Underground capitalism is flourishing in the Soviet Union; it compensates for what the Soviet State and its centralized, planned economy cannot give the population. Of the many diverse forms of activity within the Soviet underground economy, the most typical include private enterprise activity, bribery, and speculation.

The most enterprising among the Soviet people become entrepreneurs of sorts in the alternative economy by organizing unregistered private businesses. Such enterprises often emerge upon the foundation of a state enterprise or cooperative. They usually manufacture identical or similar products and use materials and supplies stolen from the enterprise. Workers in league with one another will reduce the amount of material put into the enterprise's product and use the same material for manufacturing their own product which will usually be of higher quality. The underground enterprise's product is brought to state stores and cooperative trading organizations to be sold. Additional examples of free enterprise activity abound. Enterprising students buy men's shirts, tear off the Soviet labels, sew on new colorful labels and sell the shirts as imported. Profit per shirt may be as high as 10 rubles. In the Georgian Republic a group of friends working in the garment industry opened a private storehouse where they stocked fabrics. With their stolen store of materials they began to produce their own products using a state factory. During the day the factory produced low-quality swimsuits to be sent to state and cooperative stores for sale. At night, the factory became a capitalist establishment, manufacturing high-quality goods to be sold on the black market.

Free enterprise has grown to enormous proportions in the construction branch of the official economy. Teams of workers including stonemasons, carpenters, and locksmiths have banded together and travel about the country. Receiving contracts from farms and agricultural establishments, they build animal pens, hot houses, and silos. Officially, these teams of workers and their output do not exist and they are not included in statistical data. In reality, a large share of agricultural construction can be attributed to their efforts. Moreover, all houses built for private use and all dachas are built by these independent construction teams. Materials are usually stolen from state building sites. Free enterprise in agriculture is also widespread. Workers on state and collective farms are allotted small plots of land to be farmed for their own use. They sow the crops that are most in demand and they sell most of the harvest at a profit. They devote most of their attention and labor to their private plots rather than the huge fields of state-owned farms. Furthermore, farm workers benefit from keeping animals that produce milk, eggs, and wool, which are often sold to the general public at extremely high prices until restrictive action is taken by the government.

Free enterprise practices exist within the system for supplying materials and equipment to industrial enterprises. Typically, an enterprise develops an operational plan that specifies the quantity of product it must produce but necessary materials and supplies may be lacking. To avoid being held responsible for failure to fulfill its plan, the enterprise creates a new position. It hires an unofficial purchasing agent from among the most resourceful and inventive of its workers and countenances whatever steps he may take (usually illicit) to procure the necessary materials. He will determine who has the scarce resources and trade for them, exchanging sheet metal for pipes, car hoods for cables, timber for glass, or rubber for cement. In this way an enterprise can adapt to the actual conditions of production and offset the inadequacies of central planning. There is even a market for informative talk in the Soviet Union. Someone privy to a valuable piece of news (where shoes, sweaters, coats, or any scarce goods are being sold) will take a stroll in an area where people tend to gather. As if whispering to himself, he will inform those nearby that he knows something. If they are interested, he will disclose the tidbit for a fee; his news will invariably be correct.

Bribery is a common practice at all levels and within all areas of political and economic life in the Soviet Union. The variety of situations calling for a bribe is endless: one usually needs to give a bribe to enroll in an institute or trade school, to receive an apartment, to obtain permission to travel abroad, to secure a place in a sanatorium or hospital, and, finally, to reserve a plot in a cemetery. Bribes can terminate legal proceedings. Bribes can bring a better job or promotion. Bribes do not have to be given in money; reciprocal favors or goods that are in short supply will often suffice.

To obtain a job selling *kvas*, a popular Russian beverage, to become a beer vendor, or if pumping gas is one's ambition, a bribe will be required. But the chances for personal profits later will be excellent. Beer and kvas vendors conserve for their own future use by diluting the beverages and by not completely filling their customers' glasses. The gas attendant will save the best grades for himself and dilute what he sells with cheap gasoline. Bribes often tempt those in important positions as well. A recent case involved a man who had at one time been the purveyor for the General Secretary of the Communist Party and had thus been responsible for meeting the culinary needs of Leonid Brezhnev. Although such a position has many rewards, the man who occupied it, Yuril Sokolov, had found other, illegal sources of income. He was accused of illegally accepting over 1.5 million rubles in bribes. Punishment for his crimes was execution.

Speculation is a criminal act which consists of buying goods at low prices and then reselling them at high prices. The Soviet economy, with its habitual shortages of consumer goods, is a hotbed of speculation. As a result of these shortages Soviet citizens must sign a waiting list and wait from one to two years to purchase items such as furniture, appliances, and cameras in an ordinary store. For impatient consumers, however, there is an alternative. Speculators, in collusion with store directors and sales personnel, will sell the desired goods immediately; of course the cost is much higher than the official price. The difference between the official price and the speculator's price goes into the pockets of the speculator and those in the store who abetted him. Other highly desirable items such as books, record albums, watches, and theatre tickets may also be purchased through speculators at increased prices.

All forms of private initiative in the Soviet Union formerly violated the law but recently the limited economic reforms of perestroika have permitted some free-enterprise activities to come above ground. In the past the Soviet government was actually ambivalent toward private enterprise activity. What takes place within the underground economy is tightly interwoven with the official economy. If the government ever eliminated all underground economic activity, the official economy would never be able to respond to the demands placed upon it. Thus, the Soviet government monitors illegal economic activity very carefully knowing that uncontrolled private enterprise activity could overwhelm the official economy and weaken a political system which relies on planned, centralized economic control. From time to time the government has restrained the activity of the underground economy and the growth of free enterprise by seizing its most flagrant practitioners and selectively executing the most notorious. These continuing prosecutions over many years, however, have erased the necessity and usefulness of free-enterprise activity from the thoughts of many Soviet citizens. Mikhail Gorbachev has attempted to move the government toward greater acceptance of free-enterprise activity but popular ignorance and resistance and the difficulties of combining the features of capitalist and socialist economic systems have hindered many economic reform efforts.

CRIME AND PUNISHMENT

The Soviet government does not publish statistical information about crime. If such statistics were favorable it would be expected that Soviet propagandists would not hesitate to cite them as an obvious achievement of Soviet authority operating within a socialist society. Soviet laws provide judicial bodies with the power to arrest and charge Soviet citizens at any time for violation of laws governing economic activity. Such sweeping authority has allowed the government to suppress undesirable political activity. The government can charge someone with an economic crime to avoid generating the attention that a political arrest would create.

Some acts considered crimes in the Soviet Union are crimes within the general norms of human behavior: forgery, robbery, receiving and selling stolen property. Other crimes have arisen begotten by the nature of socialism: private enterprise, speculation, the use of position for personal advantage. The Soviet criminal code contains articles designating penalties for activities considered criminal in most societies and penalties for activities considered criminal only under conditions of socialism. Soviet legislators have developed a lengthy list of statutes that aim to restrict or halt economic activity regarded as undesirable by the government. Even though current Soviet economic and political reforms have and will affect the country's civil and criminal codes, it is difficult to predict the direction and extent of future changes. Imprisonment as currently described in the statutes implies being jailed during investigation of a crime and serving the term of the sentence in a labor concentration camp, officially referred to as a corrective work camp. A selection of articles extracted from the Criminal Code of the Russian Soviet Federated Socialist Republic[2] appears in Appendix A; extracts relating to private enterprise activity, speculation, and bribery are shown below:

Engaging in private enterprise or acting as a middleman in commercial transactions (Article 153)—Free enterprise activity involving use of the state's or society's enterprises and resources; acting as a middleman in commercial transactions with intent to make profit. Penalty: imprisonment up to three years with confiscation of property or exile for a period up to three years.

Speculation (Article 154)—Stocking and resale of goods and other objects with intent to make a profit. Penalty: imprisonment up to seven years with confiscation of property.

Receiving bribes (Article 173)—Receiving directly or through an intermediary, bribes for acting on behalf of the person giving the bribe or refraining from acting to the benefit of the person giving the bribe. Penalty: imprisonment from three to fifteen years with confiscation of property and subsequent exile for a period of two to five years; violations with aggravating circumstances are punishable by execution with confiscation of property.

Giving bribes (Article 174)—Penalty: imprisonment from three to fifteen years with confiscation of property and subsequent exile for a period of two to five years.

Implication in bribery (Article 174)—Being an intermediary in the giving or receiving of bribes. Penalty: imprisonment from two to fifteen years with confiscation of property and subsequent exile for a period of two to five years.

Those charged with committing economic crimes are usually charged under several articles of the criminal code at the same time. This is understandable as private enterprise activity is almost always accompanied by theft of state property, bribery, working at prohibited occupations, or speculation. Those convicted are sent to labor concentration camps to serve the sentence of the court. Prisoners are confined to the camps and often deprived of the right to be visited by their families. They live on slim rations and must perform hard labor. The millions confined in concentration camps have become a source of cheap labor that the State Planning Committee of the Council of Ministers relies on as an integral part of the national economic plan. A shortage of prisoners is eliminated by lawfully increasing arrests, charges, and convictions. The majority of prisoners are kept in concentration camps rather than prisons since creating new camps costs little: Several thousand prisoners, under tight security and menaced by guard dogs, are transported to a remote location; a large tract of land is fenced off with barbed wire and watchtowers are erected; guards armed with machine guns man the towers; the prisoners build barracks for themselves and heated huts for the guards. When the camp begins to operate, prisoners build new cities, railroads, highways, and canals. They lay pipes for oil and gas, construct industrial facilities, and mine mineral ores and uranium. The workday lasts from ten to twelve hours; the workweek is always six or seven days.

The living conditions in Soviet labor concentration camps are very difficult. The worst of hardships is the deliberate starvation of prisoners. In all camps the amount of food provided depends on the amount of work done. Work quotas are set extremely high, beyond the strength of most prisoners. A prisoner who does not meet his work quota or who violates camp regimen may also lose visiting privileges, be denied warm clothing, and be confined to a punishment cell. Prison officials also have more subtle ways of making life insufferable for prisoners. They purposely foment mutual distrust and animosity, often based on nationality, and urge prisoners to inform on one another. Many prisoners ultimately engage in hunger strikes or commit suicide. The authorities conceal the cause of death and refuse to surrender remains to victims' families for burial.

Unfortunately, crime blights many advanced societies. It is unfair to discuss crime as an aberration peculiar to socialism. But since the founding of the Soviet Union, Marxist and Leninist ideologues have assured the Soviet people that crime is characteristic of exploitative societies, especially capitalist societies. They declare that the factors engendering crime disappear from a socialist society in which the consciousness of the people rises above the degraded level of crime and where poverty and need no longer plague the population. These conditions do not exist in the Soviet Union today and it is apparent that, after decades of Soviet leadership, crime has not vanished, only its character has changed. It is ironic that it has been the practice of private enterprise and other forms of illegal economic activity that have provided additional support to the official Soviet economy saving it thus far from ultimate collapse.

7

Objectives and Standardization of Soviet Accounting

THE EMERGENCE OF SOVIET ACCOUNTING

Accounting may be discussed in a broad geographical sense. It includes accounting and bookkeeping as they are understood in the United States and an accounting activity prevalent in the Soviet Union called *operative record keeping* which involves careful daily observation of economic transactions and immediate analysis of these transactions to determine their effect on the enterprise. Operative record keeping systems emphasize in-kind rather than monetary indicators and measurements; their use and design depend on the needs of the enterprise. Accounting itself as a function can be characterized as all-embracing and monetary. It is considered all-embracing because an enterprise's comprehensive records include all economic transactions that have occurred. It is a monetary function because, even though all kinds of measurements are used, all economic activity is ultimately evaluated in monetary terms.

After the Russian Revolution the Soviet government nationalized the economy, converting the means of production into state property. The intention of the Communist Party, when it took over the country and the economy, was to create a completely new system of centralized economic management. This system was not completely clear at the time in the minds of Party leaders, but they were determined to concentrate complete authority and power over the national economy within their hands. Planning and accounting were considered essential instruments of economic control and were to be used as part of a comprehensive system of control over the entire country.

Pre-revolutionary economics and accounting specialists provided the foundation for the development of Soviet accounting. Russians who made a contribution to the theory of accounts include Sivers in 1902, Barats in 1905, and Calagan in 1910. Some pre-revolutionary works published in France and Germany were also influential. The post-revolutionary period of accounting has produced several notable theorists as well: Galperin, Pomazkov, Kiparisov, and Dembinski. Foreign works translated into Russian and studied in the Soviet Union include those by Sher, Kalmes, Gerster, Harrison, and others. An important event in the development of Soviet accounting theory occurred in 1929. Returning from an international conference on accounting in New York, the Soviet delegation brought home a book by George Harrison on the subject of standard costs in accounting. Standard costing methods were adapted to the special features of the Soviet economic and management system. Soviet accountants then referred to the method as "the Soviet advanced method of accounting for production costs."

Accounting theory and practice in the Soviet Union were built on the foundations of theory and practice used in many countries, from tsarist Russia to industrialized early twentieth-century America. It must be stressed, however, that in borrowing the theory and practice of accounting as used in other economic systems, Soviet accounting specialists improved the borrowed theories and practices while modifying them to fit the uniqueness of the Soviet economy. The result was a qualitatively different form of accounting. In its present form the theory and practice of Soviet accounting presents much that is new and worthy of the attention of accounting specialists in other countries. The most well-known Soviet accounting theorists of the last thirty years include Vedernikov, Dmitriev, Isakov, and Margulis. We should also remember the valuable contribution to Soviet accounting theory and practice of one man now residing in the United States, the famous Soviet scholar and scientist, Dr. Aron Katsenelinboigen (Wharton School, University of Pennsylvania).

THE STRATEGIC OBJECTIVES OF SOVIET ACCOUNTING

The objectives of accounting have been modified significantly under the Soviet regime. The state views accounting as essential not only for traditional ends, such as observation and recording of financial transactions, but also for other important economic matters: To enable enterprises to obtain more favorable economic results and to develop methods which would more efficiently exploit material, labor, and monetary resources. Furthermore, since the state uses accounting data in its management of enterprises, the state has the ability to stimulate the development of enterprises in directions that satisfy the aims of the Party's Central Committee. The two primary objectives of Soviet accounting may thus be redefined and redescribed as follows: The first is traditional and descriptive—the observation and recording of economic events, followed by generalization and classification of the information obtained; the second function is active and manipulative—control and influence over economic processes with the purpose of advancing these processes in desired directions. Special significance is attributed to the second objective. Soviet authorities do not wish to regard accounting as a means of passive observation and recording.

The government has used accounting information to manage both individual enterprises and the national economy and to assist in implementing the policies of the Communist Party.

Accounting theory and practice in the Soviet Union contribute to the fulfillment of the general responsibilities of the government and the nation's enterprises. These responsibilities include the development and fulfillment of operational plans and budgets; promoting the economical use of resources; safeguarding state property; observing the principles of enterprise self-support; subordinating workers to the singular discipline of the state; and enforcing the role of the Communist Party in the Soviet economy. Accounting systems have provided Party leaders and managers of each enterprise, administrative office, and ministry with information indispensable to their mission of systematically controlling the fulfillment of operational plans and influencing enterprise activity on a day-to-day basis. This is an important element of Party administration. The significance of accounting under conditions of state ownership of the means of production is so great that the Soviet government and the Communist Party relied on accounting theory and practice as the safeguard of their political and economic domination. Such has been the strategic goal of accounting theory and practice in the Soviet Union.

These intentions notwithstanding, during the entire period of Soviet authority, central planning and an all-embracing accounting system have not become totally effective means of economic control. Economic laws and natural forces typical of free-enterprise economies inevitably interfere with the development of the socialist economy which the state's economic plans seek to achieve. Chronic shortages of materials and machinery, low labor productivity, and flagrant mismanagement and irresponsibility invariably lead to failures in meeting planned goals; thus, planning becomes ineffectual. Accounting personnel respond by altering accounting records so that managers of enterprises, administrative offices, and ministries can escape responsibility for failure to fulfill plans. Accordingly, they continue to receive bonuses and privileges for plan fulfillment.

It seems that the functions of Soviet accounting are contradictory since the observance and recording of economic events are offset by their concealment and misrepresentation. Economic results at the enterprise level are affected by efforts of enterprise management to show results in accordance with the enterprise's economic plan. Until recently, at the state level, a broader form of deception took place: Efforts were made to present economic data in such a way that socialism, communism, and the economy appeared in a favorable light, the aim being to shape public opinion both at home and abroad. Economic data were concealed and manipulated in the process. The financial statements of Soviet enterprises continue to distort actual results in varying degrees by generally overstating indicators of labor productivity and production volume. These inaccuracies are compounded within statements of the various branches of industry and in statements of economic results for the national economy. Misclassification and misrepresentation of information usually occurred without restraint at the national level. Even after exercises in manipulation, Soviet authorities often displayed a dubious self-laudatory view of the economy. But factual data concerning the Soviet economy have never been gathered. No one in the Soviet Union, including those who collect and generalize economic data, knows the actual economic condition of the country. Thus, it may be said that Soviet accounting systems have not been effective as conduits of accurate economic information.

The use of accounting systems as instruments for preventing and detecting enterprise mismanagement and safeguarding state property has resulted in more complicated systems as new and improved techniques evolve. The number of accountants in the Soviet Union is continually increasing. At present there are about three million with 85 percent of them working directly with accounting compilations and account maintenance. The system of accounting and financial control, together with the system of criminal justice, has been moderately effective in safeguarding state resources from waste, theft, and mismanagement. It is certain that, in the absence of strict control, loss of government property would increase to such a degree that it would be impossible to compensate for such losses even with a dramatic growth in production.

SOVIET INFORMATION AND THE USE OF COMPUTERS

There is no simple answer to the question "Is it possible to believe Soviet economic information?" Soviet sources provide some information that is factual and other information that is clearly overstated or understated. One may believe information on expenditures for salary funds, the amount of money in Soviet bank accounts, and the amount of outstanding bank debt. One cannot rely on information relating to the introduction or implementation of new industrial capacity or to the output and quality of Soviet products; such information is always exaggerated. Data in other areas are habitually understated: the remainder of unfinished product and the depreciation of plant assets. Some information is either fictionalized or grossly distorted: data on the completion of construction projects or the amount of arable land.

It is not possible to draw an accurate picture of the state of the Soviet economy, the condition of a particular segment of industry, or the economic activity of an individual enterprise. At the cost of much effort and time, an expert auditor acquainted with Soviet procedures for maintaining accounting records is able to make allowances for Soviet accounting ploys and derive more meaningful information. The Central Committee of the Communist Party and the State Planning Committee of the Council of Ministers know that the economic information of ministries and administrative offices is not accurate. When it is necessary to determine the actual economic results of a particular operation, basic economic indicators are reexamined and corrected by the application of a specifying coefficient. This coefficient is less than one so that exaggerated levels will be reduced. Of course, the results of such reexaminations and corrections are not completely reliable, but they are more so than the original data.

The penchant for secrecy and distortion of information has hindered the introduction of computers into the management systems of Soviet enterprises. Arguments raged for more than two decades concerning their potential use. Why Soviet reluctance to exploit computer technology in enterprise management? Distortion of information is "a delicate art done by hand." Even more important, the use of computers could result in inadvertent disclosures of information; pressing a few buttons could reveal a mass of data which Soviet authorities wished to keep secret. Thus, Soviet authorities have been extremely reluctant to utilize computer technology, yet without it, the development of the Soviet economy has been continually retarded. Another factor hampers the processing of economic information as copying machines are almost nonexistent in the Soviet Union. The government restricted normal use of such machines, considered everyday tools in Western countries, because it feared the dissemination of political documents by its opponents. But as the economy has continued to decline and perestroika reforms are implemented, joint ventures with Western companies are beginning to bring rapid technological change: thousands of personal computers have been imported from the United States and Soviet software developed for them; numerous office and factory automation systems have been installed.[1]

CENTRALIZATION AND STANDARDIZATION OF ACCOUNTING

Soviet accounting theory and practice embrace the entire economic system of the country. Accounting systems register the results of efforts to fulfill plans by individual enterprises, by segments of industry, and by the national economy. Soviet accounting methodology must therefore provide a uniform system that supplies comparable information. The uniformity and comparability of accounting data are essential in order to accomplish the following objectives: comparison of the data of individual enterprises or segments of industry with data at the national level; comparison of the data of one or a group of enterprises or one segment of industry with data for similar entities; and generalization of data for industries, administrative offices, ministries, regions, republics, and the national economy. Thus, the state strictly regulates accounting practices at every level of the national economy. State regulation of accounting and the uniformity of the accounting system are written into the Soviet constitution.

The government bodies that guide and manage accounting theory and practice in the Soviet Union are the Central Statistical Administration of the

Council of Ministers and the Ministry of Finance of the Council of Ministers. The former handles theory, the latter methodology. These bodies act in concert in administering the accounting system of the country. It is compulsory for all Soviet enterprises and their accounting departments to abide by the decisions and instructions of these organizations. The result is identical accounting procedures for all branches of the economy except budget organizations and institutions, foreign trade and military organizations, and consumer cooperatives. The ministries responsible for specific branches of the economy may propose changes in accounting forms and methods and they may formulate their own instructions, but any such changes are permitted only with the authorization of the Central Statistical Administration and the Ministry of Finance.

The Central Statistical Administration and the accounting division of the Ministry of Finance specify the following for all Soviet enterprises: the composition of monthly, quarterly, and annual reports and the terms for submitting them; the format for all accounting records; specific accounting procedures, utilizing the double-entry system for recording all transactions; and auditing practices and methods of analysis for statements and reports prepared by enterprise accounting departments. The preparation of new statement formats and accounting forms together with manuals describing their use is also the responsibility of the Central Statistical Administration and the accounting division of the Ministry of Finance. Research personnel, distinguished educators, and experienced accountants participate in drawing up such materials. The standard forms and manuals are then printed in bulk for distribution to accounting departments throughout the country.

The identification (chart of accounts) and correspondence of accounts are also standardized in the Soviet Union. This means that all enterprises use identical accounts and identical combinations of corresponding accounts for recording entries for the same kinds of transactions. The identification system for accounts requires that each account have a title and a numerical code. This system of designating accounts is officially published and is well known to all accountants, bookkeepers and managers. The combinations in which accounts are permitted to correspond are illustrated in Appendix B, the Schema of General Ledger Account Correspondence. The practical use of the double-entry system of accounting in the Soviet Union differs from its use in the United States. In the accounting system of American organizations combined or compound entries (debiting and crediting of several accounts in one entry) are permitted and even encouraged, whereas their use in the Soviet Union is avoided, being allowed only when one debit is balanced by several credits, or when one credit is balanced by several debits.

Standardization of accounting in the Soviet Union provides a number of advantages. It simplifies calculation techniques, provides a standard for accounting forms, registers, and statements, and makes it easier to prepare both individual and generalized statements and reports. These advantages are most beneficial in accounting for large amalgamated enterprises that have several affiliates. In the United States such centralization and standardization would undoubtedly be advantageous for large companies, especially for external users of their published financial information. The time may be appropriate for centralization and standardization of accounting for such multifaceted businesses. Considering the assets they possess, the capital at their disposal, the number of people employed, their annual sales revenues, and the profits they earn, each such corporation represents an industrial empire. The largest companies in America have begun, in many ways, to resemble socialist enterprises; some display the very shortcomings and vices that afflict Soviet enterprises.[2]   The authors do not question the formation of such large companies, but believe that Soviet centralization and standardization of accounting have produced procedures that could be useful to large American companies, and their Western European counterparts as well, in their efforts to improve comparability and usefulness of financial data and enhance managerial decision making.

Efforts directed toward comparability of accounting theory and practice have become more important as the countries of Western Europe approach 1992. As the European Community attempts to remove economic barriers to finance and trade, the alternative accounting practices of the countries directly affected are being closely examined. Recently the International Accounting Standards Committee has considered the importance of reducing alternative accounting practices. The IASC has reviewed the accounting practices of several nations as they relate to inventory valuation, intangibles amortization, and research and development expenditures. The IASC's recommendations for improvement in comparability of accounting practice have been published for consideration.

ACCOUNTING SPECIALIZATION WITHIN THE ECONOMY

Specialization within Soviet accounting practice results from variations in economic activity within different branches of the economy. Some areas of accounting specialization are noted:

1. Industrial accounting for machine-building, shipbuilding, mining, chemical and food production, light manufacturing;
2. Accounting for the capital investments of construction enterprises and independent builders;
3. Accounting for transport organizations providing rail, water, motor, and air service;
4. Accounting for organizations maintained on the state budget including state agencies, educational institutions, and hospitals;

5. Accounting for foreign and domestic trade organizations;
6. Accounting for military organizations and departments;
7. Accounting for labor concentration camps.

In the Soviet Union there are programs that train accountants to specialize in various branches of the economy. There are also programs that retrain accountants for new specializations or provide them with additional training in their present specialization. It may be many years before the economic reforms of perestroika produce broad changes in the theory and practice of accounting, especially at the enterprise level. But the strategic objectives of Soviet accounting must change to reflect related legal, economic, and social changes. Maybe in the future, accounting for an enterprise's stockholders' equity will become familiar practice for the Soviet accountant.

II

ACCOUNTING THEORY AS THE BASIS FOR CREATION OF ACCOUNTING PRACTICE

The development of accounting theory, the use of common accounting methodology, and the necessity for verification and control are characteristic of accounting systems that have evolved in the Soviet Union and many other countries. The use of the double-entry system for recording transactions and the balance sheet for reporting economic resources and the sources of their formation are as important for a Soviet enterprise as for any other. The Soviet economic accounting system is unique, however, because it emphasizes substantiation and standardization; this emphasis is developed and explained in Part II.

8

Development of Accounting Theory and Systems

THE DEVELOPMENT OF ACCOUNTING THEORY

In the absence of a theoretical basis, accounting becomes a skilled trade or craft. A scientifically based theory of accounting reveals the methodological bases used to reflect economic events and processes. These foundations arise from the requirements of inevitable economic phenomena. Having developed as a result of the generalization of centuries of practice in the collection and processing of economic information, the evolution of accounting theory has become the means for the further development of accounting practices.

In the opinion of Soviet specialists, mastery of the theory of accounting must always precede study of the complex and diverse practice of accounting. The mastery of accounting theory uncovers the history, objectives, goals, subject matter, and methodology as well as the general principles inherent in the accounting discipline. Proper mastery of accounting theory provides a sound understanding of accounting techniques and a sensible and creative approach to the completion of fundamental accounting tasks. A knowledge of accounting theory arouses interest in accounting practice, expands professional viewpoints, and thus promotes the further improvement of the discipline. The following goals support the development of accounting theory:

1. Continuous improvement of the general conception or notion of accounting and the understanding of its objectives;
2. Definition of the subject matter of accounting and determination of the most appropriate means to be used to achieve the objectives of accounting;
3. Development of theoretical principles for the methodology of accounting for diverse forms of movement and change in enterprise resources and the origins of those resources;
4. Determination of the general basis for creation of accounting records and procedures for compiling and presenting them;

5. Selection of the most rational accounting methods and
   techniques for their practical implementation;
6. Formation of general principles for organization of accounting
   tasks emphasizing standardization within reasonable limits;
7. Continuous improvement of accounting practices on the basis
   of theoretical research and experience both in the home
   country and beyond its borders.

Unfortunately, in most countries insufficient attention is given to development of accounting theory. This reduces accounting to the level of a skilled trade. Although recognition is hereby given to the current series of *Statements of Financial Accounting Concepts* developed by the Financial Accounting Standards Board in the United States and to the increasing efforts of international accounting theorists, accounting literature is often of a textbook nature and is intended for student use. There are almost no monographs or scientific research on the development and implementation of accounting theory. Creative discussions on theoretical problems are exceedingly rare. The absence of a theoretical basis adversely affects accounting practice. Disorder exists in the definition and classification of many concepts and an endless number of contrasting opinions appear and disappear because of the absence of serious theoretical foundations.

The explanation of accounting theory in this chapter is presented in summarized form. Only those aspects of Soviet accounting theory that might be of interest to American readers are presented and explained. Soviet doctrines, often found in accounting textbooks and monographs, that extol Soviet economic policy, criticize the free-enterprise system, and assail capitalist economies and accounting are omitted. Writings in these areas suffer from a lack of objectivity and have been directed toward strictly propagandistic objectives.

THE HISTORICAL ORIGINS OF SOVIET ACCOUNTING

In medieval feudal societies farming and trade expanded and diversified. A corresponding growth in the significance of economic accounting as a means of control and influence over these feudal economies took place. The increased importance of the role of economic accounting, the expansion of its sphere of operation, and the development of trade, culture, and science all contributed to the improvement of accounting technique and methodology. Already in the thirteenth century the double-entry system of accounting had arisen in the major commercial cities of Italy. Benedict Cotruli was the first to describe the double-entry rule. In his book *On Trade and the Honest Merchant* he included a chapter —"On the Manner of Keeping Commercial Books"—devoted to a description of the double-entry system that was in use in the shops of Italian merchants. Cotruli's book was written in 1458 but it was not published until 1573. Thus, mathematics professor Luca Pacioli is considered the first whose work on the double-entry system appeared in print. His book *The Totals (Sum) of All Arithmetic, Geometry and Calculation on Proportions and Relationships* included a section called "On Accounts and Records" and was published in 1494. The work of Benedict Cotruli, Luca Pacioli, and other scientists, generalizing the practice of economic accounting, promoted the further improvement of its technique and methodology. In feudal Russia the development of accounting was greatly influenced by Western European accounting practice and by research in accounting methodology that appeared in Russia in the eighteenth century. Economic accounting in feudal Russia was practiced by feudal lords, tradesmen and shopkeepers, clerics in churches and monasteries, and those responsible for state treasuries.

In capitalist societies the swift development of productive forces and the consolidation of production in industry and agriculture hastened the improvement of accounting procedures to meet the demands of growing economies. A rapid concentration and centralization of capital began in capitalist societies in the late nineteenth and early twentieth centuries. Naturally this affected economic accounting. Describing the basic features of capitalist accounting as it presently exists, Soviet specialists emphasize the following characteristics: the expansion of the sphere of economic accounting to match the dimensions of large economic entities; an increase in the role and significance of accounting and a corresponding increase in that of accounting specialists; the existence of an institute of certified accountants; a high level of mechanization; the absence of a definite classification of fundamental accounting categories; the absence of one, or at least several, common accounting methodologies; weak economic and theoretical argumentation for accounting processes; an inordinate fascination with complex combinations of the double-entry system; and an obsession with accounting practice and its dominating role in comparison with accounting theory. The authors do not necessarily agree with all of these conclusions but they are presented for readers' enlightenment.

THE OLD ITALIAN, AMERICAN, AND SOVIET SYSTEMS

All accounting systems are characterized by a combination of registers employed and techniques used to record entries in them. The features that define a specific accounting system include the structure of the registers, their format and mutual interdependence, and the succession and physical appearance of the entries. As the scope of world economic operations increased and they became more complicated, systems and methodologies of accounting were expanded and improved. Historically, many basic accounting systems have been developed: the Italian, the German, the French, the

American, the integral system, the card and copy systems, and the chessboard and journal-order systems. A description of each could become the subject of an independent work, so the primary features of only three (the old Venice system of Italy, the American system, and the journal-order system used in the Soviet Union) will be considered.

In the early stages of the development of trade, an enterprise's economic operations were uncomplicated. Its transactions were relatively few in number, although in scale they could be quite significant, and production still bore a trade and handicraft character. An organization or business could thus limit itself to simple accounting entries. At that time the system of accounting known as Old Italian developed and spread. A previous variation of the Old Italian system is often referred to as the Venetian system because Luca Pacioli, who described it for the first time in 1494, considered its basis the Venetian method of keeping accounts. This system of accounting was widely used in Western Europe; in small enterprises in Russia it was used until the end of the nineteenth century.

In the Old Italian system the accounting registers included three books: the Memory Book, the Journal Book, and the Principal Book. The Memory Book was a rough chronological record which was used at the moment a transaction took place. The correspondence of accounts was not indicated. Since the first record of a transaction was made in the Memory Book by the owner himself or by a trusted assistant, such a record served as the documentation and it formed the basis of the next record to be made in the Journal Book. The Journal Book was used for recording transactions based on records in the Memory Book. But it included more than a record of a single transaction as it showed corresponding accounts as well. The Journal Book also indicated the date and description of the transaction. The Principal Book, referred to as "the Notebook" by Pacioli, provided a means for systematizing entries according to debit accounts and credit accounts. Two pages were set aside for each account—the left side for debits, the right side for credits. At this stage in the development of accounting the concept of synthetic and analytical accounts[1] did not exist.   Therefore, in the Journal Book a correspondence is shown only between analytical accounts.   Pacioli recommended composing a balance sheet periodically, at least yearly, based on the entries in the Principal Book. A single person could accomplish all accounting work required by the Old Italian system. Any consideration of division of labor or segregation of duties in accounting was not relevant at this time.

The American system of accounting was proposed and developed in Europe at the end of the eighteenth century. The American system constituted an original reworking of the Italian system applied to the demands of small and medium-sized enterprises. This system became widespread in Western Europe and Russia, but not in America. The American system was normally used in enterprises having fewer than twenty-five synthetic accounts. In the American system chronological and systematic entries are arranged in one book called the Journal-principal. Placing both entries together significantly reduces the number of accounting processes. Required analytical accounting can be carried out in books or on cards. The American system of accounting, in view of its authorship and region of popularity, can be considered American in name only.

In the United States there is no single preferred system of accounting. The principle of accountability requires American enterprises to keep accounts but, in most industries, no one regulates the system or techniques utilized. Consequently, enterprises in the United States may choose any arrangement or combination of registers and any form of mutually linked synthetic and analytical accounts. The systems selected very frequently depend on the size of the enterprise, the volume of its operations, and the degree of centralization. The plethora of accounting variations used in the United States makes it impossible to describe one system that could be regarded as predominant. The majority of American textbooks point to four special journals and one general journal which are used for recording chronological entries. The possibility of using several more special journals is presented. In the United States elements of other systems, such as the card and copy systems, are also found in use in small businesses.

The majority of enterprises in the Soviet Union use the Journal-order system. This system is based on the use of accumulated journal-orders and auxiliary records that function as registers for synthetic and analytical accounts. Journal-orders are designed to reflect transactions in accordance with the principle of the chessboard entry whereby account correspondence for repetitive entries is determined in advance. In this system debit and credit entries are made in the appropriate accounts and the correspondence between them is indicated. Exceptions are for the petty cash and cash in bank accounts. For these, debit records are kept simultaneously with the journal-order credit records. The Journal-order system of accounting has important advantages. It provides for the systematizing and amassing of data from preliminary documents; it combines the chronological and systematic entry processes; it provides for the correspondence of accounts; and it reduces opportunities for error. Soviet enterprises utilize more than thirteen specialized accounting journals with the Journal-order system.

THE SOVIET ECONOMIC ACCOUNTING SYSTEM

In a broad sense the methodology of accounting consists of following and recording natural and societal phenomena and processes for the purpose of obtaining information about them. For human society keeping an account of all phenomena is important, but economic processes are of special interest. Economic processes include the constantly recurring processes of production, distribution, exchange, and consumption. At first, these processes occur within individual enterprises, then they are linked with analogous processes at the national level, and, finally, at the international level. The complex activities of industrial enterprises require the design of a system that will embrace all of the diverse economic events occurring within each enterprise and produce information required by interested parties. In the Soviet Union this is achieved by the application of operative control, accounting and statistics.

Operative control can be defined as the immediate recording of individual economic events and processes within defined sectors of an enterprise to permit daily control and management of these events and processess. With the implementation of operative control, information is received about the quantity and quality of products sold, the capacity and use of equipment, expenditures for materials, labor, and energy, the movement of unfinished goods within the factory, and compliance with economic agreements. The effectiveness of operative control may be limited by factors such as the internal structure of a specific enterprise, the inability to record transactions as soon as they occur or shortly thereafter, the use of a variety of natural and physical measurements, and by failure to assess the efficiency of resource usage.

Accounting is a special activity characterized by complete and uninterrupted observation of economic events, processes and resources, by recording only those transactions substantiated by evidencing documents, and by generalization of all information in monetary measurements. Accounting systems exist in all Soviet enterprises and institutions. The generalized data produced by them are used for characterizing the activity of all enterprises, each economic sector, and the economy as a whole. Thus, accounting can be described as all-embracing because all economic events which affect enterprise assets and their sources are recorded using a double-entry system. Accounting entries are substantiated by documentation because only those events evidenced by documents are considered. All economic events are recorded in monetary terms using the ruble as the universal measurement.

Statistics is a social science directed toward the study of the quantitative characteristics of mass events and processes in all areas of a society including its economic activity. Using specified, methodical processes such as observation and correlation, the characteristics of the economic activity of a society and its components are revealed. In Soviet industrial enterprises statistical data produced for such indicators as the volume and quality of products and the productivity of the labor force are widely used for analysis of the economic activity of an enterprise. In the Soviet Union operative control, accounting, and statistics constitute a single system of economic accounting in which data supplied by one component are supplemented by data of the other components. For example, in the contemporary arrangement of economic accounting for materials, a combination of operative control and accounting is used for control and management whereas statistics and accounting are used to formulate data for analysis.

Soviet economic accounting systems require use of natural, labor-based and monetary measurements for the quantitative and qualitative evaluation of economic resources. Natural measurements, representing physical and qualitative characteristics, are used in accounting for economic resources and for controlling quantitative and qualitative changes in them. In the Soviet Union such indices may be expressed as the number of items, meters, kilograms, and liters. Using natural measurements the quantities of items such as raw materials and finished products are determined. Natural measurements may also express certain qualitative attributes such as scale, strength, and capacity and may be simple or complex. The latter consists of two or more in-kind indices. Examples include the ton/meter index used for measuring transport work, the kilowatt/hour used for determining energy use, and the kilogram/square centimeter used for measuring pressure and strength. Occasionally, conditional or equivalent in-kind indices are applied. Canned goods can be measured by the can, with one can holding 400 grams of food substance, and fuel can be measured by its heat-conducting capacity at, for example, 7,000 kilocalories/per kilogram.

Labor-based measurements serve to determine the expenditure of labor expressed in units of time (days, hours, minutes) thus permitting calculation of the time necessary to perform a specific task. Labor indices are frequently used with in-kind indices (man-days, man-hours) to determine labor productivity and to calculate and control the fulfillment of manufacturing norms. Notwithstanding the significance in economic accounting of natural and labor-based measurements, it should be noted that the results of such calculations cannot always be generalized and compared. This is accomplished by monetary conversion of natural and labor-based measurements. The production of goods and the appearance of money gave rise to monetary measurement which nowadays is used for generalization of the dissimilar indicators necessary to measure each enterprise's economic resources and activities. The use of monetary indices thus makes it possible to correlate diverse items through their monetary value.

9

Accounting Methodology and Enterprise Resources

THE SUBJECT MATTER OF ACCOUNTING

The operation of most industrial, construction, trade, and consumer service enterprises in the Soviet Union is based on the self-support principle. In practice, this means that an enterprise must offset all of its expenses with the revenues it earns from the distribution and sale of its products and services. Furthermore, the enterprise should generate a profit, the greater part of which the government directly or indirectly appropriates. In order to carry out their operations industrial enterprises are provided with various economic resources: buildings, machinery, instruments, fixtures, raw materials, unfinished goods, fuel, and cash allocations. The allotment of economic resources by the government is always based on the minimum requirements of the enterprise. The circulation of an enterprise's economic resources proceeds without interruption within three stages: the process of provisioning, the process of production, and the process of distribution and sale. Each of these processes is characterized by numerous economic events that cause changes in the composition, form, and sources of the enterprise's economic resources.

In the process of provisioning, the appropriate departments of an industrial enterprise, in accordance with its established plan, obtain the materials, components, supplies, fuel, and spare parts required by the enterprise for normal productive activity. Obtaining such goods results in the creation of production reserves in the warehouse and the creation of payment relationships with suppliers. The production process begins as soon as materials and components are conveyed to the enterprise's production departments. The process is continued and completed through introduction of and interaction with labor and productive equipment. The output is in the form of new resources of production and objects of consumption. The production process is the most important and complex of the three processes. Costs of production are incurred within this stage of the cycle. The production process ends with the completion of the product and its transfer to the enterprise's warehouse.

The process of distribution and sale is the final stage of circulation. In this stage finished products located in enterprise warehouses are distributed and sold to consumers. Distribution and sale result in payment relationships with customers. The quality, reliability, and price of the finished product determine consumer acceptance and the results of the distribution and sale process. After the process of distribution and sale is complete, the process of provisioning begins again. The successive processes of provisioning, production, and distribution and sale continue throughout the life of the enterprise.

The circulation of economic resources of industrial enterprises comprises two spheres: the sphere of production, which includes the process of production, and the sphere of exchange, which includes the process of provisioning and the process of distribution and sale. Each successive cycle of economic resources normally exceeds the volume of the preceeding cycle; this occurs since production proceeds in accordance with the economic law of continuous expansion. The economic resources of industrial enterprises are simultaneously involved in all three stages and both spheres of circulation.

During circulation, as an enterprise's economic resources pass from one stage to another and from the sphere of production to the sphere of exchange and back again, they also undergo changes in form. Thus, cash resources used to obtain materials, components, supplies, and fuel are converted to other goods indicating movement from the sphere of exchange to the sphere of production. Items incomplete at one stage of production are passed through additional operations and are then moved to the warehouse in the form of finished products to be distributed and sold. As such, the enterprise's economic resources pass from the production sphere to the exchange sphere; after distribution and sale they assume once again the form of cash.

At every stage in the circulation of economic resources innumerable economic operations occur. Each represents an elementary, one-step action and an individual and specific accounting event. It is important to be able to precisely define the limits of each economic operation and correctly evaluate its economic significance. The complexity and variety of economic operations and the constant movement of economic resources demand continued attention and close control. The subject matter of accounting thus includes a determination and analysis of the following for each enterprise: the existence and origin of its economic resources, the changes in volume and composition of those resources, the enterprise's economic activity, and the financial results of that activity.

THE METHODOLOGY OF ACCOUNTING

Every science is equipped with its characteristic methodological devices. In accounting several devices constitute its methodology: documentary substantiation, inventorying, evaluation, calculation, recordkeeping using the double-entry system, and generalization of economic information in a balance sheet and other statements. Documentary substantiation of accounting entries requires that an economic operation be based on a document in order to be recorded in the accounting records. Documents accepted by enterprise accounting departments as substantiation must be composed in accordance with specified formats and display all required attributes. Inventorying is the determination of the quantity of economic resources at an enterprise's disposal by means of physical item counts and measurements; also necessary is the subsequent comparison of counted or measured results with acccounting records. Variances are then determined and their causes investigated.

Evaluation is the description of economic resources, the sources of their formation, and economic processes by means of a monetary indicator. Use of this methodological device makes it possible to translate inventoried amounts into monetary values thereby providing information for generalization and comparison. As a consequence the enterprise can then determine the financial results of its activity. Calculation is the process of determining the enterprise's cost for each unit of product produced and for operations and services performed; the cost is expressed using monetary indicators. Calculation is used to determine numerous other costs such as the cost of fuel consumed and the cost of salaries paid. Recordkeeping by means of the double-entry system demands that each economic operation be expressed with amounts affecting at least two accounts simultaneously. Generalization of economic information in a balance sheet and other statements enables the enterprise to summarize and report information, using monetary values, about the availability and disposition of its economic resources. This information is used for control and analysis.

Use of the methodological devices enumerated above provides a complete, continuous, interrelated, and documented presentation, expressed in monetary and in-kind values, of enterprise economic resources and processes. Therefore, accounting methodology should be considered an aggregate of methodological devices by means of which the subject matter of accounting is reflected objectively in reports which are useful for control and analysis. In the expanded description of accounting methodology that follows in this and later chapters, each of the aforementioned methodological devices is explained in detail. Since generalization of economic information in a balance sheet is at the foundation of accounting theory and practice in the Soviet Union and the United States, this device will be explored first. To obtain an accurate perception of the structure of a balance sheet for a Soviet enterprise, one must possess at least an elementary knowledge of the manner in which economic resources and the sources of their formation are classified in Soviet accounting literature.

ECONOMIC RESOURCES OF AN INDUSTRIAL ENTERPRISE

The economic resources of an industrial enterprise are divided into three basic groups: plant assets, circulating assets, and assets beyond circulation. Plant assets (buildings, structures, fixtures, machinery, equipment, instruments, tools, vehicles) are used repeatedly. They retain their original configuration and wear out gradually. Their original cost is written off periodically in proportion to their utilization. Circulating assets are completely consumed and transformed in the production process. Their cost is included in production costs as soon as they are utilized. Circulating assets may be classified as limited and unlimited. The reserves of limited circulating assets must be constantly maintained within established norms. Limited circulating assets include low-cost expendable items, materials, components, supplies, spare parts, fuel, and finished and unfinished products. Unlimited circulating assets include cash resources, accounts receivable, and shipped goods; amounts and quantities held are not subject to limitation.

In the classification of economic resources certain means of production occupy an intermediate position between plant and circulating assets. Items such as tools and instruments, costing less than 100 rubles per unit regardless of service-life, or assets whose service-life is less than one year irrespective of cost, are considered low-cost expendable items. These resources function as plant assets in economic processes, but their service-life, low cost, and the nature of their use make it appropriate to regard them as circulating assets. The inclusion of low-cost expendable items in the classification of circulating assets has the advantage of simplifying accounting procedures by making it easier to include their cost in the enterprise's cost of production. Assets beyond circulation, usually cash resources, are withdrawn by the government in anticipation of profits. These assets are actually withdrawn from the enterprise but remain on the balance sheet until formally transferred to the state budget or written off at year-end. This retains the actual amount of enterprise net income for year-end analysis.

An industrial enterprise's economic resources are obtained from various sources which are classified within three groups: fixed, borrowed, and allotment obligations. The fixed sources of economic resources provide those the enterprise receives from the government through responsible state agencies. The primary fixed source of assets is the State Equity Fund; assets come to the enterprise in the form of material resources and cash. A supplementary fixed source of economic resources is the state budget. This source is described as Financing from Budget. The budget financing is provided for replacement of plant assets and replenishment of circulating assets. Budget financing is considered a fixed source because it remains at the disposal of the enterprise and subsequently becomes part of the State Equity Fund.

Enterprises create an amortization fund for capital repairs and the replacement of plant assets by adding a monthly amount to the cost of production. The amortization fund, which in part remains at the disposal of the enterprise, is also considered a fixed source of economic resources. The economic activity of an enterprise, based on the self-support principle, is generally profitable. The greater portion of an enterprise's net income is transferred to the state budget at the end of the accounting period, but a small part remains at the disposal of the enterprise and serves as another fixed source of economic resources. The Funds for Economic Stimulation, created by the enterprise by allocation from its net income and also from savings gained by reducing production costs, is yet another fixed source of economic resources.

The borrowed sources of economic resources are represented by short-term and long-term loans from state banks. Bank credits are allocated only for strictly defined purposes. Short-term credits are provided to cover reasonable enterprise requirements for additional circulating assets. Long-term credits, with a term of more than one year, are granted for capital investments connected with the development, improvement, and modernization of production processes. All forms of indebtedness arising from payment relationships with other enterprises are also regarded as borrowed sources of economic resources. Allotment obligations that result from allocation of the national income are a specific source of asset formation. The allotments arise from the enterprise's continuing salary obligations to its employees and its payment obligations to the state budget and social security organizations.

The classification of enterprise assets and sources of their formation is based on Karl Marx's economic theory. This classification is followed for all accounting, planning, and statistical activities in the Soviet Union and all countries in the Eastern Bloc. Figure 9.1 presents the classification of economic resources (assets) and the sources of their formation (state equity and liabilities) for a typical Soviet industrial enterprise.

Figure 9.1
**Classification of Economic Resources and Their Sources
in a Soviet Industrial Enterprise**

Assets	State Equity and Liabilities
Plant Assets	**Fixed Sources**
Buildings and Structures	State Equity Fund
Power-generating Equipment	Financing from the State Budget
Transmission Mechanisms	Amortization Fund
Production Machinery and	Retained Net Income
Equipment	Funds for Economic Stimulation
Measuring, Regulating and	
Laboratory Equipment	**Borrowed Sources**
Transport, Conveyance and	
Loading Vehicles	Short-term Bank Loans
High-priced Tools and Instruments	Long-term Bank Loans
Fixtures and Similar Plant Assets	Accounts Payable
Other Plant Assets	
	Allotment Obligations
Circulating Assets	
	Amounts Due for Employees'
<u>Limited</u>	Salaries
Low-cost Expendable Items	Amounts Due to the State Budget
Materials and Supplies	Amounts Due to Social Security
Purchased Semifinished Products	Organizations
Spare Parts for Machines	
Fuel	
Work in Process	
Finished Products	
<u>Unlimited</u>	
Shipped Goods and Completed	
Work	
Cash Resources	
Accounts Receivable	
Assets Beyond Circulation	
Net Income Withdrawn by the	
State	
Net Losses	

Source: Derived from standard forms developed by the Soviet government for
use by all industrial enterprises.

10

The Balance Sheet, Account Theory, and Verification Devices

THE BALANCE SHEET AS AN ACCOUNTING DEVICE

Economic resources of an enterprise and the sources of their formation are subject to constant movement and changes in form. The results of these events within specific time periods is continuously recorded and monitored. The balance sheet is the most important display of this activity. Balance sheet preparation is a procedure widely used in planning and accounting to establish certain correlations: revenues and expenditures and the availability of resources and their allocation. The illustrative balance sheet of a Soviet industrial enterprise appears in condensed form in Figure 10.1; a complete balance sheet would have over 200 items. The presentation, using only monetary values, of enterprise economic resources according to their allocation and the sources of their formation constitutes the most important function of the balance sheet. In this respect the balance sheet of a Soviet enterprise looks identical to the balance sheet of an enterprise in the United States. This resemblance, however, is superficial. A balance sheet reflects the typical features of an enterprise operating within a particular economic system. Thus, the Soviet balance sheet will reflect the salient feature of the Soviet economy, namely, state ownership of the means of production[1].

As seen in Figure 10.1 the Soviet balance sheet differs from that used in the United States in description and classification of items. The Soviet balance sheet always shows assets on the left and liabilities on the right. The order in which individual items are listed within these sections differs from that found on an American balance sheet. The order of items on the asset side of the Soviet balance sheet is designed to underscore the enterprise's strengths, whereas the order of items on the liability side indicates the priority of claims to the assets. The claims of the state are always presented first.

Contrary accounts on the balance sheets of Soviet enterprises, as on American balance sheets, were displayed on the side of the balance sheet where the account regulated by the contrary account is located. During the last

Figure 10.1
Balance Sheet of a Soviet Industrial Enterprise (abbreviated)[a]
Assets (rubles in thousands)

Composition and Distribution of Economic Assets	Limits[b]	Line No.	Amount	Common size %
A. Plant Assets and Assets Beyond Circulation				
1. Plant (Fixed) assets (01)		01	297,400	58.5
2. Withdrawn assets (Net income distributed) (81)		09	72,400	14.3
3. Losses (Debit balance, Account 80)		13, 14	-	-
Total in Section A		15	369,800	72.8
B. Limited Circulating Assets				
1. Raw materials, supplies and purchased semifinished products (05)	21,810	17, 18, 20	28,870	5.7
2. Fuel and combusible materials (06)	310	19	440	0.1
3. Spare parts for plant assets (08)	420	21	820	0.2
4. Low-cost expendable items (12)	13,360	22	43,180	8.5
5. Work in process (20, 21, 23)	23,400	25	26,550	5.2
6. Prepaid expenses for future periods (31)	1,000	28	420	0.1
7. Finished goods and nonmanufacturing expenses (40, 43)	8,000	29	6,180	1.2
Total in Section B	68,300	35	106,460	21.0
C. Cash Resources, Debtors and Other Assets				
1. Cash resources:				
Petty cash in the office (50)		36	-	-
Cash in bank (51, 55, 56)		37	12,050	2.4
2. Goods shipped and services rendered (45)		45, 46, 47	10,430	2.1
3. Accounts receivable (Debtors) (61, 63, 70, 71, 73, 76, 77, 78, 79)		54, 60, 61 62, 66	750	0.1
4. Capital repair expenses (03)		70	4,190	0.8
5. Other assets		71	4,320	0.8
Total in Section C		72	31,740	6.2
D. Resources and Expenses of Capital Construction (Total)		73	-	-
Total Balance (Lines 15 + 35 + 72 + 73)		75	508,000	100.0

Source: E. T. Astashkevicher (E. Ash), Accounting for a Machine-Building Plant (Moscow: Mashinostroenie, 1970), 346-48; substantial changes in Soviet accounting forms and procedures occur infrequently.
[a]The numbers in parentheses after each item correspond to the official chart of accounts for industrial enterprises.
[b]Minimum levels required to be maintained in accordance with government norms.

Continued on next page.

Figure 10.1 continued
Liabilities (rubles in thousands)

Sources of Formation of Economic Assets	Line No.	Amount	Common size %
A. Basic Sources of Assets Allotted to the Enterprise			
1. State equity fund (85)	76	247,170	48.7
2. Accumulated depreciation (02)	78	80,450	15.8
3. State budget financing (85)	80	-	-
4. Net income before distribution (80)	87	73,910	14.6
5. Stable liabilities:			
Salary and insurance premiums payable (69, 70)	89	4,600	0.9
Reserves for future expenses and payments (89)	90	1,540	0.3
Total in Section A	98	407,670	80.3
B. Bank Credits toward the Acquisition of Limited Circulating Assets			
1. Loans for circulating assets (90)	99	31,840	6.3
2. Loans for materials and fuel (90)	100	660	0.1
3. Loans for finished goods inventory (90)	102	980	0.2
Total in Section B	107	33,480	6.6
B-1. Depletion of Low-cost Expendable Items (Total)(13)	108	31,480	6.2
C. Various Bank Loans and Other Liabilities			
1. Short-term bank loans (90)	117	11,900	2.3
2. Long-term bank loans (92)	119	4,130	0.8
3. Accounts payable (Creditors) (60, 63, 76, 77, 78, 79)	130, 137	6,480	1.3
4. Special funds and financing for special purposes (87, 88, 96)	138, 139	12,230	2.4
5. Amortization fund at the disposal of the enterprise for major repairs (86)	142	630	0.1
Total in Section C	148	35,370	6.9
D. Sources for Capital Construction (Total)	149	-	-
Total Balance (Lines 98 + 107 + 148 + 149)	152	508,000	100.0

few decades the practice has been changed. Contrary accounts on a Soviet balance sheet are now placed on the side of the balance sheet that is opposite that on which the regulated account is located. Accumulated depreciation is located on the liability side of the balance sheet, while the related asset item is placed on the asset side. Accounting for the specific contents of the balance sheet is explained in the chapters in Part III.

ACCOUNTS AND THE DOUBLE-ENTRY SYSTEM

As in the United States, a preliminary grouping or arrangement of the results of economically similar financial transactions is attained through the maintenance of accounts. By keeping accounts, continuous control can be maintained over economic processes and the allocation and movement of economic resources and the sources of their formation. An account is thus opened and maintained for every type of economic resource and for all sources of economic resources; accounts are opened for some separate financial operations as well. In general Soviet practice, an account consists of a table divided into two parts on a card, a sheet of paper, or a page in a book. One part of an account is conventionally called the debit side and the other part is known as the credit side. Contemporary accounting practice features use of automated systems for maintenance of accounts.

Recording in accounts in the Soviet Union as in the United States employs the double-entry system. Accounting theory reveals the philosophy and methodology of the double-entry system as follows: On the debit side of one account and on the credit side of another, at one and the same amount, every economic transaction is recorded; the two entries (in debit and credit) take place simultaneously and are mutually dependent. The double-entry system thus represents the two changes that every economic transaction causes in the composition of economic resources and/or the sources of their formation. Double-entry bookkeeping is one of the fundamental devices of accounting methodology. About five centuries have passed since the principles of the double-entry system were first explained in accounting literature. Over the course of time the double-entry system has changed only in form; innumerable accounting records throughout the world are maintained in accordance with its principles. Since theory and practice operating over the course of several centuries have not produced a better approach, it is apparent that the existence of the double-entry system rests on reasons of an objective nature independent of the will or desire of man.

The aim here is not to present an account of every existing theory of double-entry accounting but it is fitting to provide at least a brief description of the most notable justification for the double-entry system. Among all theories of the double-entry system three stand out: one based on judicial principles, a second based on economic principles, and a third based on accounting principles. In the judicial approach every economic operation is regarded as a legal or judicial act in which one party receives something and another gives something. This act creates an obligation for the receiving party and a right for the giving party. In other words, the party that receives something is obliged to the party that has given something; and the party that has given something has rights against the party that has received something. The entire economic activity of a party involved in the transaction consists of its either receiving or giving something, and this produces either the right to receive something or the obligation to return what was received. Hence, in accounting for economic acts, it is absolutely necessary to indicate the giver and the recipient, what has been given, and the reason for the transaction. Consequently, the duality of legal relationships engenders the duality of accounting.

The economic approach views every economic operation as a process of cost exchange in which one cost is exchanged for another. This theory must be considered simultaneously with the judicial relationships expressed previously. In Soviet accounting the inferences derived from the economic approach are more significant. In the accounting approach the basis of every entry is considered to be its effects or influence on the balance sheet. It is this approach that is adhered to in the United States. Every economic operation has a corresponding influence on the structure and content of the balance sheet. In the United States special significance is attributed to this influence. The classification of accounts, the accounting records, the technique of itemizing—everything is subordinated to the effect of an economic transaction on the balance sheet. Highly desirable results might be attained if one could manage to combine the economic approach to the theory of double-entry accounting with the accounting approach. Then every economic operation occurring in an enterprise would be regarded as a process of cost exchange and as a factor affecting the structure and content of the balance sheet.

SOVIET ACCOUNT CLASSIFICATION

The arrangement of accounts based on their economic content is of the essence since it makes possible correct usage of the innumerable accounts existing in practice. Although all accounts have a specific designation, many of them have general characteristics that enable the accountant to arrange them in groups. Such an arrangement of accounts on the basis of their economic content is called *account classification*. Within the study of accounting theory the classification of accounts has great significance. It facilitates the correct recording of entries and the retrieval of information. The study of account classification fosters a mastery of the methodological device of double-entry accounting. Soviet accounting theory and practice provide a carefully developed classification of accounts and stipulate a range of accounts that are available for use. In this respect Soviet accounting can be considered highly standardized. It is considered necessary that the student of accounting master and apply account classification before beginning to study transaction recording using the double-entry system.

Soviet account classification is based on the economic content of accounts; the primary consideration is the economic essence of transactions to be recorded in the accounts. In accord with this premise all accounts are divided into five primary categories:

1. Accounts for economic resources (Asset accounts),
2. Accounts for sources of formation of economic resources (Liability and Equity accounts),
3. Adjusting accounts (contrary and supplementary),
4. Accounts for economic processes,
5. Accounts for final financial results.

Each of these primary categories is further divided into smaller groups and subgroups. In the Soviet Union a detailed description of each category, group, and subgroup is carefully studied.

For purposes of uniformity, comparison, and consolidation, the Soviet Union uses a single chart of accounts[2] containing the title of each account, its numerical code, an explanation of the use of each account, and the interrelation and correspondence among accounts. The official chart of accounts, with the comprehensive manual for its use, is published in a special book of more than 300 pages. The single functional chart of accounts for all Soviet enterprises is composed by the Ministry of Finance in agreement with the Central Statistical Administration. The chart consists of nine parts, each of which contains accounts of the same economic group. In addition, the chart of accounts includes a group of Off-Balance-Sheet Accounts designed for accounting for resources that do not belong to an enterprise and are therefore not presented on its balance sheet. All recording in Off-Balance-Sheet Accounts is made by single entries in each account.

Appendix C presents a summary of the chart of accounts now used by Soviet industrial and construction enterprises. In the Soviet Union there is complete uniformity in recording of specific entries under the double-entry system; only designated accounts may be used to record specific transactions.

INVENTORYING AND DOCUMENTARY SUBSTANTIATION

In order to maintain accuracy of accounting data and records, it is necessary to periodically check accounting data and records against the actual state of economic resources and payment relationships; this is accomplished by inventorying. Inventorying is thus a verification of cash, property and other economic resources, payment relationships, and other sources of resource formation. Factual data acquired in verification are compared with accounting data and records and variances identified. All variances determined in the course of inventorying are recorded in appropriate accounts. Surpluses are entered in the accounts for which they were uncovered, but shortages are recorded in a special account and subsequently become the subject of further analysis and possible investigation.

The development of economic activity and the related increase in the number of transactions stimulated documentary substantiation of accounting entries. This occurred after the double-entry system came into use. In the fifteenth century when the double-entry system was first used, the basis of an entry for a transaction was its ink record in the draft ledger. At that time economic transactions were registered in the books without strict documentation; the records themselves had the status of documents. Even in the fifteenth century there was a tradition of considering trade ledgers as a special type of document. It should be mentioned, though, that in Luca Pacioli's time certain documents such as bills of exchange and business correspondence were in use among the merchant class. Pacioli, in his tract on accounting, mentioned these documents and even suggested a system for organizing and preserving them. Nevertheless, he never coordinated them with account entries.

Documents remain separate from accounting records in Pachiolo's work. Accounting records themselves had the force of proof or evidence if they were kept in accordance with accounting rules. In court investigations documents corroborating the accuracy of accounting records were unnecessary. This situation furthered the practice of undocumented registration of economic operations in commercial books for a long period. As the elevated legal status of accounting records continued, abuses and malfeasance in recordkeeping began to develop. Consequently, trade books and ledgers began to lose their former trustworthiness. The aim of documentary substantiation of accounting entries was to restore that trust; thus began the practice of referring to an appropriate document for every entry in the ledger. Other factors also promoted the development of documentation in accounting. First, entrepreneurs, during their periods of absence, began to entrust their business affairs to assistants who were obliged to prove the accuracy of records maintained during such absences. Second, as trading companies developed, the capital of many entrepreneurs was combined; entrepreneurs began to require substantiation of every accounting entry with an appropriate document to obtain accurate information about the results of their undertakings.

In accounting literature in the United States the principle of documentary substantiation does not receive as forceful a treatment as in Soviet literature. In the Soviet Union great significance is attached to documentation. A detailed classification of documents is, as a rule, found in textbooks end manuals. The presence of a document supporting each and every economic operation is obligatory. An approximate account of what is published in Soviet manuals about accounting documentation follows.

The necessity of showing that an economic transaction has been carried out in a correct, expedient, and legal manner arises not only when the transaction takes place, but after it has taken place as well. Thus, entries for economic transactions in accounting registers and the periodic verification of accounting records must be based on and corroborated by documents. Documentary substantiation of economic transactions is one of the most important requirements of accounting. It fosters the security of assets, provides for the availability of reliable data on the work of the enterprise, and imparts to accounting the force of proof. All documents must contain certain data known as requisites. Several of them are required on every document: the document title; the place and date of preparation; an indication of the parties taking part in the transaction; the basis, content, and indicators (in-kind and monetary) of the economic operation; and the signatures of those who carried out the transaction and recorded it. Most documents also have a serial number.

Document circulation is the term used to describe the flow of a document from its creation through its signing, movement, processing, and passage to archive storage. The accounting department of a Soviet enterprise plans and controls document circulation to ensure that it occurs within specified time periods. The department verifies data on originating/source documents and also determines the corresponding accounts for each accounting entry before recording it in one of thirteen special journals. Such recording procedures provide the accumulation and classification of documentary data that is essential for account maintenance and statement preparation.

III

ACCOUNTING FOR ECONOMIC RESOURCES, THEIR SOURCES, AND ECONOMIC PROCESSES IN SOVIET INDUSTRIAL ENTERPRISES

Industry in the Soviet Union consists of more than 46,000 enterprises linked to one another by economic relationships resulting from diverse and complex economic processes. Many financial transactions are completed in the course of a day in every industrial enterprise. Enterprises acquire various objects of production and, using the means of production at their disposal, the enterprises then manufacture products to be distributed and sold. In an industrial enterprise the entire process of economic resource circulation is an endless and often complicated process of exchange and renewal. This process and other economic events are described in enterprise accounting records that must be maintained in the manner prescribed by the state. Part III presents the recording, reporting, and analysis of economic resource circulation for Soviet industrial enterprises.

11

Accounting for Plant Assets

OBJECTIVES OF ACCOUNTING FOR PLANT ASSETS

In industrial enterprises plant assets include a much greater portion of total economic resources than in other types of enterprises. Since the plant assets of Soviet enterprises form the economic basis of Soviet industry, much importance is attached to accounting for and control over them. Accounting for plant assets should provide for:

1. Control of their security by means of documentary substantiation and timely accounting for their availability and movement;
2. Timely and accurate completion of all documentation for transactions involving plant assets;
3. Precise calculation of amortization (depreciation) and correct reflection of these amounts in the accounting records and as a component of the enterprise's cost of production;
4. Control of the planning and performance of capital repair of plant assets;
5. Preparation of information necessary for analysis of the efficiency of use of plant assets, especially equipment.

The organization and techniques of accounting for plant assets in the Soviet Union is influenced by Soviet economic policy, which fosters extremely long periods of use. Most Soviet enterprises are equipped with unproductive and obsolete equipment; some machines are used for twenty, thirty, or more years. The level of mechanization of labor-intensive work is very low. This is because human labor in the USSR, especially unskilled labor, is cheaply valued. Consequently, the introduction of machinery to replace such labor proceeds slowly. Various resolutions of the Party and government concerning the question of better equipping enterprises are often of a propagandistic nature:

they are not prompted by economic considerations. These circumstances affect accounting for the availability and utilization of plant assets.

CLASSIFICATION, VALUATION, AND CONTROL

The characteristics of plant assets include prolonged (longer than one year) use in production cycles, a unit cost higher than the established limit (currently 100 rubles), uniform inclusion of their cost in total enterprise manufacturing costs according to wear suffered in the production process, and repair, renovation, and replacement carried out by utilization of special funds. Assets not possessing these characteristics are considered circulating assets. In the Soviet Union the classification of plant assets has exceptional significance: The single approach to classification provides for uniform treatment by all industrial enterprises. Plant assets may then be divided into two primary groups on the basis of their use in the production process: Plant assets are considered either productive or nonproductive.

Productive plant assets are those which the worker uses to alter directly the objects of production during the manufacture of the product. Assets such as buildings and other structures that provide the conditions necessary for the production process are also classified as productive plant assets. Productive plant assets are subdivided into the following groups on the basis of their function in the economic activity of the enterprise: (1) buildings; (2) various structures and installations such as fuel tanks, pipelines, and platforms; (3) power-generating equipment; (4) output transmission mechanisms; (5) production machinery and equipment; (6) measuring and regulating devices and laboratory equipment; (7) tools; (8) materials handling equipment; (9) various production accessories such as work tables, shelving, and boxes; (10) work animals and landscaping and land reclamation equipment. Uncultivated land, forest plots and underground resources do not have cash value in the Soviet Union and are considered using natural measurements beyond the balance sheet. Nonproductive plant assets are not utilized in the production process; they are utilized in providing consumer, cultural, medical, and social services. Included are buildings, furnishings, and equipment utilized by schools, libraries, hospitals, and child care centers.

Buildings must be completed with equipment installed before they are considered plant assets. Free-standing machines and equipment, equipment requiring assembly but intended for permanent use, and other items having the characteristics of plant assets become part of an enterprise's plant assets when they are received by the enterprise. A distinction is made between an enterprise's own plant assets, permanently installed in the enterprise, and those leased from other enterprises or organizations. Plant assets that are leased are accounted for by the using enterprise in an off-balance-sheet account called Leased Plant Assets; they are not reflected on the balance sheet because they are already on the balance sheet of the enterprise leasing them. Only capital investments in leased plant assets can be considered within the plant assets of an enterprise.

When evaluating plant assets an enterprise must distinguish original cost, replacement cost, and residual cost. The original (historical) cost of plant assets is the cost derived from expenditures for their construction, manufacture, or acquisition; also included are expenditures for delivery and installation. Replacement cost is the cost of obtaining plant assets of identical or similar condition and capability to those currently in use. There are situations that may require adjustment of the original cost of a plant asset: reconstruction or renovation in which discarded parts are replaced by improved parts or in which the asset is augmented with new parts that increase its worth, and discovery of errors in calculation of the original cost. Other changes occur in accordance with government reappraisal procedures that require periodic redetermination of original cost. After plant assets undergo reappraisal, replacement cost is reflected in the balance sheet if original costs are considered unreasonable.

During the lives of plant assets physical deterioration and obsolescence take place. Obsolescence occurs when assets become less valuable as more efficient assets are put into use or when similar assets can be repaired and renovated at less cost. Deterioration and obsolescence of plant assets (amortization) is calculated each month on the basis of established government norms. The appropriate portion of plant asset costs may then be included in an enterprise's cost of production. Deterioration and obsolescence of plant assets is reflected in a contrary balance sheet account called Accumulated Depreciation shown on the liability side of the balance sheet. This account is similar to the contra-asset account which appears on American balance sheets as a deduction from the cost of the related plant assets. The difference between the cost of plant assets and the amount reflected for deterioration and obsolescence is referred to as the asset's residual cost (book value).

Account 01, Plant Assets, is used to account for the receipt, disposition, and internal transfer of plant assets. Plant assets are reflected in this account on the balance sheet at documented original cost. The deterioration and obsolescence of plant assets is reflected in Account 02, Accumulated Depreciation. This account indicates increases in amortization as credits and decreases in amortization as debits. An analytical account is maintained for each separate plant asset inventory unit. Each unit may be simple or complex (several connected units) and will include the asset and all accessories and components considered part of its cost and necessary for operation of the asset. For example, considering buildings, an inventory unit refers to each structure that stands separately including its communication, electrical, heating, plumbing and sewage systems; its maintenance equipment; and its elevators. Referring to machinery and equipment, an inventory unit includes the basic mechanical unit with its stand or other mounting parts, its regulating devices, electrical circuitry, and any other components included in its overall cost. The composition of every plant asset inventory unit is defined in its technical documentation.

A serial number is assigned to every inventory unit as soon as it is put into use or placed on reserve as a spare unit. The assignment of serial numbers fosters safekeeping and simplifies accounting. The number remains assigned to the unit until it ceases to be part of the plant assets of the enterprise; the same number is not assigned to new units. Enterprises using many plant assets of the same type are required to maintain an analytical account on inventory cards utilizing formats established by the government for separate groups of plant assets. A special invoice record form is used for internal transfer of plant assets within the enterprise. Entries for internal transfer of plant assets are made only within analytical accounts.

ACCOUNTING FOR AMORTIZATION (DEPRECIATION)

Plant assets gradually wear out and/or become obsolete. Each month amortization is calculated so that a portion of the cost of plant assets corresponding to their deterioration and obsolescence may be included in the enterprise's cost of production and the decrease in real worth of plant assets may be deducted from the enterprise's liabilities to the state. Amortization is charged for all enterprise plant assets except land, producing and work animals, technical libraries, and plant assets temporarily out of use. The calculation of amortization is based on norms set by the government. The norms are differentiated according to separate types and groups of plant assets but they are used by all Soviet enterprises and organizations. The norms are established as percentages based on the original costs of plant assets and are set separately for complete renovation or replacement (capital investment) and partial renovation or modernization (capital repair). The norms are contained in a manual published by the State Planning Committee for use by enterprise accounting departments.

For most plant assets amortization is calculated and charged monthly. When plant assets are received by an enterprise amortization is first calculated and charged in the following month; for plant assets leaving the enterprise amortization ceases in the month following removal of the asset. An amortization fund is thereby formed and designated for financing of capital investments and capital repairs. The amount of amortization calculated for the month is credited to Account 86, Amortization Fund, and appropriate analytical accounts. It is then distributed accordingly among the cost-forming accounts: For plant assets used in auxiliary departments the amortization is debited to Account 23, Auxiliary Departments; for production equipment and tools the amortization is debited to Account 24, Expenses for Use and Maintenance of Equipment; the amortization sum for factory buildings is divided among departments and debited to Account 25, Departmental Manufacturing

Overhead; the amortization sum for buildings of general use is debited to Account 26, Factory Manufacturing Overhead.

The expenses of auxiliary departments, expenses for use of equipment, and departmental and factory manufacturing overhead will be included in the cost of production and become an integral part of it. The portion of amortization that relates to nonproductive plant assets will be debited to Account 29, Nonindustrial Facilities and Departments; this amortization will be omitted from the cost of production. The compound entry for amortization of plant assets for each month will show the following debits (Dr.) and credits (Cr.):

Dr. Account 23 Auxiliary Departments
Dr. Account 24 Expenses for Use and Maintenance of Equipment
Dr. Account 25 Departmental Manufacturing Overhead
Dr. Account 26 Factory Manufacturing Overhead
Dr. Account 29 Nonindustrial Facilities and Departments
    Cr. Account 86 Amortization Fund

The inclusion of amortization of plant assets in the cost of production and the creation of an amortization fund is accompanied by another entry that shows an identical increase in the accumulated depreciation of an enterprise's plant assets and an identical decrease in the State Equity Fund. Thus, the second entry will be as follows:

Dr. Account 85 State Equity Fund
    Cr. Account 02 Accumulated Depreciation

The amortization of plant assets does not reduce the original cost of plant assets directly. It diminishes the obligations of the enterprise to the government for subsidies received. The process of recording depreciation of plant assets in the Soviet Union differs from that utilized in the United States. The primary difference is that Soviet enterprises not only calculate and record depreciation, but also accrue an amortization fund for renewal of plant assets through renovation or the acquisition of new units. The depreciation of plant assets in the USSR is calculated using only two methods: the straight-line method and the units-of-output method; accelerated methods of depreciation are not used. Depreciation of plant assets in Soviet enterprises continues as long as the asset is in use, often for long periods since plant assets (in civilian enterprises) are replaced much less frequently than in American enterprises. Thus, the estimation of service lives for plant assets and the establishment of uniform and strict norms of depreciation lose their significance in the Soviet Union. They would be more meaningful in the United States where the use of a plant asset is often limited to its predetermined service life. The fact that amortization of plant assets in the USSR is calculated and charged to the cost of production for the entire period of their use may be explained thus: If the creation of the amortization fund ceased or were interrupted, a Soviet enterprise would lose its single source of plant asset renovation or acquisition. The high cost of repairs often absorbs significant portions of amortization fund balances. The differing approaches to the calculation and recording of depreciation in the United States and the Soviet Union are thus reflected in the costs of their manufactured products and the financial results of their enterprises.

ACCOUNTING FOR REPAIR OF PLANT ASSETS

Work intended to restore the operational capabilities of plant assets is called repair. It is customary to distinguish capital repairs from routine repairs by reference to the volume, nature, and duration of the work. Repairs that require replacement of all worn-out parts or several of the most important parts of a plant asset are considered capital repairs. For buildings, structures, and other installations involved in production, repairs are regarded as capital when worn-out components are replaced by new and efficient items that improve operational capabilities without entirely replacing the fundamental structure. For machinery and equipment, repairs are considered capital when the machine is dismantled and all worn-out components are replaced or restored and other components are repaired. Capital repair of machinery and equipment takes place infrequently as a rule, not more often than once a year. Repairs for transport vehicles are regarded as capital when they are carried out after the vehicles have been used for specified distances within the working conditions established by government experts. Account 03, Capital Repairs, is used for accounting for the cost of capital repairs. All expenditures for capital repairs are recorded on the debit side of this account regardless of whether they were carried out by the enterprise itself or by an independent contractor.

Capital repairs on equipment, machinery, and transport vehicles are usually carried out in special repair and mechanical shops of an auxiliary department. In such cases expenditures are first accumulated in a cost-forming account, Account 23, Auxiliary Departments. The cost of separate parts removed from plant assets during capital repair and intended for future use is removed from Account 23, Auxiliary Departments, and debited to corresponding accounts. This reduces the cost of capital repairs previously entered in Account 23. In order to motivate enterprises to repair their worn-out and obsolete plant assets, they are permitted to write off the actual cost of capital repairs against the marketable product output. Therefore, the cost of capital repairs that the enterprise completes itself is transferred from Account 23, Auxiliary Departments, to Account 46, Sales, and then to Account 03, Capital Repairs. Thus the actual cost of capital repairs will be recorded by two entries:

1. Dr. Account 46 Sales
       Cr. Account 23 Auxiliary Departments
2. Dr. Account 03 Capital Repairs
       Cr. Account 46 Sales

     The cost-flows through Account 46, Sales, which will be illustrated more fully in a following chapter, are the most important indicator of enterprise economic activity; they characterize fulfillment or nonfulfillment of the technical-industrial-financial plan. However, these cost-flows include those for capital repairs. Consequently, in analyzing the marketable product output of a Soviet enterprise, one must make allowances for these costs which cannot be regarded as related to the marketable product. The cost of capital repairs of buildings, installations, and other permanent structures is not written off against the marketable product output. They are transferred from Account 23, Auxiliary Departments, directly to Account 03, Capital Repairs, by-passing Account 46, Sales.
     As already indicated, a specially designated portion of the amortization fund constitutes the primary source of financing for capital repairs. Upon completion of capital repairs on plant assets and the resumption of their use, all costs of repairs recorded in Account 03, Capital Repairs, are entered as reductions of the amortization fund. The following entry will record this transaction:

Dr. Account 86 Amortization Fund
       Cr. Account 03 Capital Repairs

After capital repairs are completed, the accumulated depreciation account is decreased accordingly and obligations to the state increased by the same amount. This is accomplished by the following entry:

Dr. Account 02 Accumulated Depreciation
       Cr. Account 85 State Equity Fund

     In certain circumstances the government permits enterprises to acquire new plant assets using the amortization fund. In such cases expenditures made for acquiring, delivering, and installing new plant assets are regarded as capital investments and are recorded by the following entry:

Dr. Account 86 Amortization Fund
       Cr. Account 51 Cash in Bank

The placement of these plant assets into operation is reflected by the following entry:

Dr. Account 01 Plant Assets
    Cr. Account 85 State Equity Fund

Since no capital repairs were completed, the accumulated depreciation account shows no reduction for the cost of the newly acquired units.

Expenditures incurred for routine repairs, those that are carried out regularly, are grouped as debits to Account 23, Auxiliary Departments. Upon completion of the repairs, their cost is transferred from Account 23 to Accounts 24, 25, and 26 depending on the type of plant asset repaired. If the cost and volume of routine repairs vary substantially from month to month, the actual costs from Account 23, Auxiliary Departments, will be debited first to Account 89, Reserves for Future Expenses and Payments, and then allocated in installments to Accounts 24, 25, and 26. The repair of plant assets is one of the most complicated and difficult problems faced by Soviet enterprises. The poor quality of machinery and equipment results in frequent breakdowns, long-idle periods, and costly repairs. As a rule, there are insufficient spare parts; many replacement parts are made on the spot by hand. The quality of such parts is very low while their cost is exceptionally high. These circumstances are reflected in the accounting process. Since the high cost of completed capital repairs is written off as a reduction to Account 02, Accumulated Depreciation, the amount of plant asset amortization reflected on the liability side of the balance sheet is usually very small. So the longer a unit is used and continuously repaired, the lower its accumulated depreciation. This creates the illusion that the plant assets of Soviet enterprises are new or in just-purchased condition.

ACCOUNTING FOR ACQUISITION AND DISPOSAL

The acquisition of plant assets represents an inflow of economic resources increasing the obligations of a Soviet enterprise to the state; this transaction increases the balance of the State Equity Fund account. Plant assets are usually received by an enterprise as a result of capital investment, but also from uncompensated conveyances from other enterprises at the order of government authorities. Capital investment is carried out by enterprises either through construction, manufacture, or acquisition of plant assets. Most enterprises have separate accounting procedures for capital investment, which are in addition to the accounting procedures for the enterprise's principal activity. Thus, an industrial enterprise will prepare two sets of financial statements, one for its principal activity and a second for its capital investment transactions. The accounting for capital investments includes all transactions relating to asset cost and sources of financing. When the process of construction, manufacture, or acquisition is completed, the assets become subject to the accounting procedures for the enterprise's principal activity. A distinguishing feature of the Soviet economic system is the gratuitous transfer of plant assets from one enterprise to another. Since the resources of all enterprises are the property of the state, the transfer of plant assets among enterprises does not involve payment. Only in the exceptional circumstances of a state enterprise obtaining a plant asset from a cooperative organization does payment take place.

The receipt of plant assets as a result of capital investment or their gratuitous transfer from other state enterprises or organizations must be accompanied by a conveyance document. The receipt of a plant asset with an original cost of 3,800 rubles will be reflected by the following entry:

Dr. Account 01 Plant Assets   3,800 rub.
    Cr. Account 85 State Equity Fund   3,800 rub.

The receipt of the plant asset increases both the amount of the enterprise's resources and its obligation to the state. If the plant asset is not new its current amortization is used to increase the credit balance of Account 02, Accumulated Depreciation, and decrease the amount recorded by the previous entry in Account 85, State Equity Fund. This is shown by the following entry:

Dr. Account 85 State Equity Fund   900 rub.
    Cr. Account 02 Accumulated Depreciation   900 rub.

As a result of these entries the balance in Account 01, Plant Assets, increases by 3,800 rubles; the balance in Account 02, Accumulated Depreciation, increases by 900 rubles; the balance in Account 85, State Equity Fund, increases by 2,900 rubles (3,800 − 900), which corresponds to the residual cost of the asset received.

Disposal of plant assets results from one of the following actions: gratuitous transfer to another enterprise at the order of government authorities; discarding of those that have fallen into disrepair or lost their productive value; sale with permission of government authorities of those no longer needed. When an enterprise disposes of a plant asset it must first calculate its amortization since the amount is not determinable from accounting records. The amortization for each plant asset unit is determined on the basis of its original cost, the duration of its use, the norms for amortization provided by the government, and the cost of capital repairs made to the asset. This information is obtained from records maintained for each plant asset inventory unit.

The disposal of plant assets due to gratuitous transfer to other enterprises is officially registered in a receipt-transfer agreement between the enterprises involved. Two entries will reflect this transaction in the synthetic accounts of the transferring enterprise:

1. To remove the original cost of the transferred unit:
        Dr. Account 85 State Equity Fund
            Cr. Account 01 Plant Assets
2. To remove the amortization of the transferred unit:
        Dr. Account 02 Accumulated Depreciation
            Cr. Account 85 State Equity Fund

The entries for the gratuitous transfer of plant assets are opposite those recorded for the gratuitous receipt of plant assets. Both receipt and disposal of plant assets affect the obligation of the enterprise to the state through the State Equity Fund: receipts increase the obligation while disposals reduce the obligation.

Plant assets that have lost their productive value owing to physical deterioration as well as obsolete plant assets are subject to disposal. The discarded asset is removed from the accounting records considering its original cost and amortization, expenses incurred during disposal (dismantling, removal, etc.), and the cost of reusable materials remaining after disposal (supplies, fuel, spare parts, etc.). The cost of remaining materials will be charged to appropriate inventory accounts. Accounting for disposal of plant assets is accomplished directly through Account 85, State Equity Fund, since the disposal of plant assets affects the amount of an enterprise's obligation to the state. Whenever plant assets are disposed of a document is prepared to reflect the transaction. On the basis of the documentation, the following typical entries are recorded using the disposal of a building as an example:

1. To remove the original cost of the building:
        Dr. Account 85 State Equity Fund   12,600 rub.
            Cr. Account 01 Plant Assets   12,600 rub.
2. To remove amortization of the building:
        Dr. Account 02 Accumulated Depreciation   9,000 rub.
            Cr. Account 85 State Equity Fund   9,000 rub.
3. To record receipt of the contractor's bill for demolition:
        Dr. Account 85 State Equity Fund   300 rub.
            Cr. Account 60 Suppliers and Contractors
                                Accounts Payable   300 rub.
4. To charge the cost of materials remaining after disposal to the appropriate inventory accounts:
        Dr. Account 05 Production Materials   1,150 rub.
        Dr. Account 06 Fuel and Combustible Materials 1,250 rub.
            Cr. Account 85 State Equity Fund   2,400 rub.

The entries recorded in Account 85, State Equity Fund, reduced its balance by 1,500 rubles (−12,600 + 9,000 − 300 ÷ 2,400). Losses from the disposal of plant assets that have not been completely amortized (with the exception of enterprise residence buildings) affect the financial results of the enterprise. This will be reflected by the following final entry in the synthetic accounts:

Dr. Account 80 Income and Losses   1,500 rub.
    Cr. Account 85 State Equity Fund   1,500 rub.

In the Soviet Union neither the exchange of plant assets between enterprises nor the purchase of plant assets by trading in old ones present any special problem since such transactions rarely occur. Land and all natural resources belong to the state. Therefore, enterprises engaged in mining do not calculate amortization or depletion for the exhaustion of natural resources. Intangible assets such as patents and goodwill that sometimes appear on American balance sheets are nonexistent at the enterprise level and never appear on enterprise balance sheets.

12

Accounting for Materials
and Low-Cost Expendable Items

THE IMPORTANCE, CLASSIFICATION, AND VALUATION
OF MATERIAL RESOURCES

Raw and processed materials, semifinished components and accessories, manufacturing supplies, packing materials, fuel, spare parts for plant assets, and other material resources are considered the objects of production in the manufacturing process. Accordingly, as they are consumed or utilized, their costs become part of the cost of the products manufactured by an enterprise. The cost of materials is the largest component of production costs in a Soviet industrial enterprise. In machine-building enterprises materials costs account for about 60 percent of all production costs, while in other industries they account for as high as 90 percent of all production costs. Costs for materials make up such a large proportion of the expenses of a Soviet industrial enterprise because the cost of labor is extremely low.

Official planning bodies, which must anticipate what will be needed for uninterrupted operation of the production process, establish limits on the material reserves kept in enterprise warehouses. In practice, however, Soviet enterprises suffer chronic shortages of critical materials while surpluses of other, often unnecessary, materials frequently occur. When a plant or parts of it stand idle due to shortages, items that are in short supply are frequently replaced by unsuitable substitutes that lower the quality and attractiveness of the product. Materials have become the most attractive items of plunder and speculation on the black market. Although penalties for stealing are severe, workers are not deterred: they display amazing resourcefulness in acquiring needed materials. To limit losses of materials due to theft or inefficient use a strict system for delivering, receiving, documenting, classifying, storing, and issuing materials has been developed. Its methods are cumbersome, but it is of definite value in limiting losses.

Materials are divided into several groups according to their function in the production process: raw and processed materials, semifinished components and accessories, auxiliary materials, packing materials, fuel, and spare parts for machines and equipment. Raw materials are those that are the products of the mining or extracting industry (coal, iron ore, oil, etc.). Processed materials are the products of a processing industry and are used by other industries to produce new products (fabrics, glass, plastics, steel, etc.). A complete official list of materials called the Nomenclature Price List includes both technical descriptions and price data. A numerical code is assigned to each material on the list. The composition of the code indicates the type of material, its technical properties, its quality and other characteristics. To account for the availability and flow of materials the following synthetic and analytical accounts are used:

> 05 Production Materials with the following subsidiary
>   accounts—(1) Raw and Processed Materials, (2) Semifinished
>   Products and Accessories, (3) Auxiliary Materials, (4)
>   Animals and Products of Auxiliary Agricultural Departments,[1]
>   (5) Packing Materials;
> 06 Fuel and Combustible Materials;
> 08 Spare Parts For Plant Assets.

Similar to other circulating assets of industrial enterprises, materials are accounted for in the balance sheet at their actual cost to the enterprise. Actual cost is derived from the sum of wholesale prices paid to suppliers and additional purchasing and transport costs. These additional costs include the following: maintaining purchasing facilities near suppliers, travel to visit supplier representatives, additional markups for suppliers required by the government, delivery charges of carriers, loading and unloading charges, and waste and loss during shipment. Thus, calculation of actual cost for each type of material may be very complicated and time consuming. For the sake of simplicity, the current accounting basis for materials is normally determined using the average annual budgeted cost of the material to the enterprise or the wholesale price of the material excluding additional costs. Wholesale prices for all materials in the Soviet Union are established by the government. Price variances between the current accounting basis using average annual budgeted cost and actual cost are computed using the following formula for each synthetic materials account:

$$
\text{Average Percentage of Variance} = \frac{\begin{array}{c}\text{Price variance} \\ \text{at beginning of} \\ \text{the month}\end{array} + \begin{array}{c}\text{Price variance} \\ \text{for the} \\ \text{current month}\end{array}}{\begin{array}{c}\text{Materials inventory at} \\ \text{beginning of the month} \\ \text{at budgeted cost}\end{array} + \begin{array}{c}\text{Materials received} \\ \text{during the current} \\ \text{month at budgeted cost}\end{array}} \times 100
$$

As an illustration, assume that on December 1 materials at a budgeted cost of 364,000 rubles remained in inventory and the price variance between actual and budgeted cost was –8,850 rubles (a favorable variance is a minus, an unfavorable variance is a plus). During December 90,000 rubles of materials were received. The price variance between actual and budgeted cost for the materials received was –2,700 rubles. Using the formula above, the average price variance percentage for the materials is 2.5 percent calculated as follows: [(–8,850) + (–2,700) × 100] ÷ (364,000 + 90,000). To determine the actual price of the materials the budgeted cost should be reduced by 2.5 percent. Regardless of the current accounting basis used, the inventory of materials on the balance sheet will be shown at actual cost. This means that if the current accounting basis is budgeted cost, the actual cost on the balance sheet will be presented as budgeted cost plus or minus the price variance; if the current accounting basis is wholesale price, the actual cost will be presented as the wholesale price plus purchasing and transport costs.

CONTROLLING AND ACCOUNTING FOR MATERIALS

Providing enterprises with necessary materials is accomplished by the State Planning Committee (Gosplan USSR), which allocates resources in accordance with the type and volume of production specified by each enterprise's technical-industrial-financial plan. All enterprises then contract for delivery of materials with appropriate suppliers on the basis of their Gosplan allocations. All materials received by an enterprise must be accepted by warehouse personnel who are responsible for completing required documentation. Warehouse personnel, especially managers, are also responsible for maintaining current information about the receipt, issue, and availability of materials. Lapses in this area are considered crimes. Most Soviet industrial enterprises employ the balance method of accounting for materials which fulfills the requirements of analytical accounting. Moreover, accounting for materials is carried out under the direct supervision and constant control of the enterprise's accounting department. The accounting department issues an accounting record card to the warehouse for each item of material. The record card includes the description, nomenclature price list code, unit of measure, accounted cost (current accounting basis), and established government inventory limit for each material. The card represents an official document that must be protected from alteration or loss.

The accounting department of a Soviet enterprise provides accounting for the acquisition, availability, and use of materials using both in-kind and monetary values. Acquisition and storage of materials is recorded on the basis of receipts and invoices from suppliers. The accounting department determines the actual cost of expended materials including both purchasing and transport costs and variances from budgeted costs; the actual cost is recorded in the appropriate accounts as follows:

Dr. Account 20 Principal Work in Process
Dr. Account 23 Auxiliary Departments
Dr. Account 24 Expenses for Use and Maintenance of Equipment
Dr. Account 25 Departmental Manufacturing Overhead
         Cr. Account 05 Production Materials

In Soviet enterprises the actual use of materials is measured by scrupulous documentary evidence. The amount of materials not on hand in the warehouse should be equal to the quantity of materials actually requested. Inventorying as a means of primary control over materials use is permissible only for low-cost bulk materials at building sites (sand, gravel, stone). In the United States inventorying is used more frequently to determine actual use of materials. The principle behind this approach is simple: the materials not on hand are considered used for production or sale. In a Soviet enterprise materials missing from the warehouse without documentary substantiation will immediately be qualified as a shortage and recorded in appropriate journals as such. Significant quantity variances and deviations from expected usage will become the subject of investigation, the consequences of which can be very serious.

Another important characteristic of Soviet accounting for materials must be considered. Soviet enterprises use only two methods for calculating the cost of inventory: the weighted average method and the specific-invoice price method. Other methods, such as FIFO (First-in, First-out) and LIFO (Last-in, First-out), as well as the gross profit and retail methods, are not used. Thus, use of various methods of inventory cost determination cannot serve as a means to affect the cost of goods sold and the net income or loss of an enterprise.

THE NATURE AND AMORTIZATION (DEPLETION) OF LOW-COST EXPENDABLE ITEMS

Economic resources that cost less than 100 rubles and have a service-life of less than one year are classified among an enterprise's circulating assets as low-cost expendable items. This category also includes the following as exceptions to the general requirements: special tools and instruments ordered on a one-time basis regardless of cost; spare machinery and equipment; special clothing, footwear, linen, and other dormitory items regardless of service-life or cost; automation devices and laboratory equipment costing less than 300 rubles and acquired by utilizing special funds available from the government. These items resemble plant assets in their economic function as means rather than objects of production but, since their cost and service-life do not permit their classification as plant assets, accounting for them is similar to that for materials. Synthetic accounting for low-cost expendable items is accomplished using Account 12, Low-cost Expendable Items.   Those retained in the warehouse are classified in Subaccount 1; those issued and in use appear in Subaccount 2. The transfer of these assets from the warehouse is recorded by an internal entry as an exchange between subaccounts.

Amortization (depletion) is applied to all low-cost expendable items issued and used. The method of amortization depends on the type of item. The following classifications exist: items of general use such as factory tools; items of special use such as a special order for military purposes; spare machinery or equipment, items costing less than two rubles each; and items acquired utilizing funds for economic stimulation or special purposes. Amortization of items having a general use is determined at 50 percent of the original cost at the time the items are issued and used. The remaining 50 percent is amortized when the items are removed from use due to deterioration or unfit condition. At that time, the amortization is reduced by the value of scrap which is charged to the appropriate materials accounts, and by the value of items lost or damaged which may be deducted from the salaries of those responsible.   Amortization of low-cost expendable items is credited to a contrary balance sheet account, Account 13, Depletion of Low-cost Expendable Items. An illustration of calculations and recording procedures for these assets for one month follows.

Assume that 3,760 rubles of low-cost expendable items were put into use: production departments received 1,900 rubles and auxiliary departments received 900 rubles; tools for use with equipment costing 960 rubles were also issued. In the same month, items costing 4,240 rubles were removed from use due to their unserviceable condition as follows: from production departments 2,100 rubles, from auxiliary departments 540 rubles, and from use with equipment 1,600 rubles. When these items were withdrawn 280 rubles of scrap was salvaged. The assets being removed from use will be valued at 3,960 rubles (4,240 – 280) and written off by a debit to Account 13, Depletion of Low-cost Expendable Items, and a credit to Account 12, Low-cost Expendable Items. A schedule of amortization of low-cost expendable items appears in Table 12.1.

Table 12.1
Amortization of Low-Cost Expendable Items

Original Cost of Items in Rubles				
1	2	3		
Transferred from Warehouse	Removed from Use	Scrap to be Reused	Amount Amortized[a]	Account Debited[b]
900	540	80	640	23
960	1,600	40	1,240	24
1,900	2,100	160	1,840	25
3,760	4,240	280	3,720	

[a]Columns 1 + 2 ÷ 2 − Column 3
[b]Account 23, Auxiliary Departments; Account 24, Expenses for Use and Maintenance of Equipment; Account 25, Departmental Manufacturing Overhead. Account 13, Depletion of Low-cost Expendable Items is credited.

13

Accounting for Labor
and Payroll

SALARY PAYMENTS AND PERSONNEL CLASSIFICATION

Salary payments in the Soviet Union are defined as the portion of the total gross national product which is allocated by the government in monetary form to workers. Salary payments are a comparatively small part of all industrial production costs. In machine-building enterprises salary payments are only about 10 percent of the production cost of the product. The use of resources allocated for salary payments is tightly controlled in the USSR. This is attributable to a rigid system of personnel classification, careful recording of time worked and output, and establishment of strenuous norms of production.

The personnel department is responsible for control of workers at each Soviet enterprise. All personnel are divided into two major groups. Permanent employees are those working at an enterprise for an indefinite time and entitled to regular remuneration and benefits. Temporary employees are hired for individual jobs, work as long as the enterprise needs them, and are entitled to limited benefits. Employees are also classified according to the nature of the work they perform within the enterprise. Employees are considered industrial workers if they participate directly or indirectly in the production activity of the enterprise. Nonindustrial workers occupy positions unrelated to production: they work in enterprise housing and community service departments and agricultural, educational, and medical organizations. Those engaged in capital repair of buildings, structures, and installations are also classified as nonindustrial personnel. All employees are further classified according to the functions they perform as follows: workers, apprentices, engineering-technical personnel, clerical, maintenance, and security personnel. The grouping of employees by function and position completes the classification of personnel within an industrial enterprise. Industrial workers and apprentices perform specific activities such as those of milling machine operator, drill operator, and metalworker. Other employees may operate as engineers, planners, accountants, and secretaries. Employee qualifications are very important for correct salary payment in the Soviet Union. Each job category has various levels of competence required. The level a worker has reached is used in determining his qualifications as are his education, work experience, and length of time worked. The overall qualifications of an employee and his political loyalty affect his assignment to a particular position and establishment of his rate of pay.

Salary payments for certain industrial workers are based on a schedule (tariff) of hourly rates established for the six official levels of competence. Hourly rates of pay depend not only on a worker's level of competence, but also on the complexity of the work, the effort it demands, and the dangers it may involve. Employee identification numbers and attendance/performance records are used by an enterprise's accounting department to determine the actual time worked or lost and to determine and record salary payments for each worker as well as the enterprise as a whole. For management, engineering-technical, and clerical workers, position pay rates are set in accordance with tables established by the Council of Ministers. The Council's position pay-rate tables are based on state norms for salary payments. The tables contain the ranges of pay rates indicating the minimum and maximum permissible salary for each position.

The funding for salary payments is the total sum of monetary resources allocated to an enterprise's workers. In planning and accounting a distinction is made between principal and supplementary salary payments. Principal salary payments are payments for time worked or for work performed. They are calculated according to tariff pay scales, piece-work rates, and position pay rates. Also included are bonuses and additional payments for night and overtime work, abnormal working conditions, loss of work time, spoilage not caused by workers, and for work as team leader or foreman. Supplementary salary payments are payments employees receive in accordance with government regulations for prolonged interruptions such as vacations and time spent studying in educational institutions. The initial basis used for calculation of salary payments may be the amount of time worked or the amount of work completed. It is important to stress that in the Soviet Union preference is given to the piece-work basis of calculation, that is, to that dependent on results of work performed rather than on time spent.

PRINCIPAL AND SUPPLEMENTARY SALARY PAYMENTS

The technical level and organization of the production process where workers perform their jobs determines the form of initial control for worker output. Regardless of the system of accounting and documentation used by a particular enterprise, the original output control document must contain certain indicators that are necessary for day-to-day accounting and technical control and for calculation of labor statistics and salary payments. These important indicators include: the document title, date of issue, and place of work; the shift, identification number, and name of the worker or team of workers; the competence level of the worker or team, job categories, and norms of output (per hour or shift); and the rate of pay per unit when the piece-rate system is applied. Also included are comments on the condition of completed output (good production accepted and spoilage separated), conditions of payment for spoilage (if applicable), the actual time worked by each worker or team, the sum of salaries to be paid, and references to any additional documents.

The Manual for Planning, Accounting, and Calculation of the Cost to the Enterprise of the Product in Machine-Building and Metal Working provides various procedures for organizing accounting and technical documentation for determining worker output. The procedure used in a particular enterprise depends on its level of production: mass output, limited edition or serial, unique or custom product. An additional accounting responsibility involves documentation and calculation of supplementary salary payments. As indicated previously, workers in industrial enterprises sometimes receive payments in addition to those for time worked or work performed. These payments are under especially strict control and require preparation of special documents, such as medical certificates, with approval indicated by signatures of authorized persons.

The most common supplementary salary payments are those for used and unused vacation time, for time spent fulfilling political and societal duties, for time used by mothers for child care, and for hours during which minors do not work but for which they have a right to receive pay (privilege hours). A worker earns the right to a regular vacation by working in a the same enterprise for at least eleven months; fifteen days is the minimum length of time for a vacation. Determination, recording, and payment of vacation payments are based on the length of time a worker has been with an enterprise and on his average salary for the twelve calendar months immediately preceding the vacation period. In specific situations fixed by law, supplementary salary payments are allocated to workers for time spent on political and societal duties. These payments are determined, recorded, and paid on the basis of average hourly salary for the three-month period immediately preceding that in which the duties are performed. Nursing mothers are paid for time used for feeding their children. When they are paid on a time-spent basis the payment is accounted for only to make a distinction between principal and supplementary salary payments. In effect, the rate of pay is identical since the full rate applies to all payments. When the piece-work method of payment is in effect the payment is determined on the basis of average hourly earnings. Workers are considered minors until they reach the age of eighteen. Soviet law establishes a shorter workday for minors, who are, however, paid for a full workday. The part of their pay received for time not worked is a supplementary salary payment.

ANALYTICAL AND SYNTHETIC ACCOUNTING
FOR SALARY PAYMENTS

All information relating to the determination of principal and supplementary salary payments and withholdings is recorded in each enterprise's payroll records. The actual amount due to an employee, as determined by the accounting department, is the sum of all earnings minus withholdings. Salary payments in Soviet enterprises are usually made twice a month. For the first half of the month, workers receive an advance equal to approximately 50 percent of their net monthly salary; the remainder is received at the end of the month. Enterprise cashiers make salary payments within a three-day period with workers signing the appropriate payment document. Analytical accounting procedures ensure that necessary information about salary payments and withholdings is obtained. Such information is maintained for each employee, for groups of workers, for departments of the enterprise, for different forms of salary payments and withholdings, and by different types of products and classifications of expenditure. Such data are used for determining an enterprise's cost of production, for determining certain supplementary salary payments, and for inclusion in various reports and reference materials. In small enterprises, where accounting for labor and payroll is not computerized, analytical accounting for salary payments requires use of manually maintained employee salary files. In the majority of large enterprises in the machine-building industry, analytical accounting for labor and salary payments is computerized.

Before salary payments and analytical account data related to them are reflected in synthetic accounts, they are grouped within several classifications: by shop, department, or other enterprise division; by employee job category or position; and by form of payment and withholding. Principal and supplementary salary payments are then reflected as debits in the synthetic accounts in the following manner: for industrial workers in production departments in Account 20, Principal Work in Process; for industrial workers in auxiliary departments in Account 23, Auxiliary Departments; for industrial workers servicing machinery and equipment in Account 24, Expenses for Use and Maintenance of Equipment; for engineering-technical and clerical personnel and unskilled industrial workers and apprentices of the shops in Account 25, Departmental Manufacturing Overhead; for management and clerical personnel and unskilled industrial workers and apprentices involved in factory management in Account 26, Factory Manufacturing Overhead; for all employees in nonindustrial facilities and departments in Account 29, Nonindustrial Facilities and Departments.

In determining the cost of production, principal and supplementary payments are treated differently. Principal salary payments are entered directly into the production cost of specific products through Account 20; supplementary salary payments are then distributed in proportion to principal salary payments. The total of principal and supplementary salary payments, entered on the debit side of the accounts listed previously, is credited to Account 70, Payroll. The credit balance of this account, reduced by amounts withheld, indicates the amount an enterprise owes to its employees as salaries.

SALARY WITHHOLDINGS AND EMPLOYEE BENEFITS

Permissible withholdings from salary payments include a tax on income; taxes on bachelors, couples without children, and small families; amounts to offset advances previously paid; fines levied by administrative and judicial bodies; amounts to pay for goods bought on credit in retail trade markets; and premiums for voluntary insurance. The amount of tax withholdings is determined by calculating a fixed percentage of salaries earned in the previous month. Resolutions of civil courts and directives of administrative bodies, including enterprise management, often determine the amount of other withholdings. Child-support payments, for example, may be deducted on the basis of a court decision or a parent's voluntary written declaration.

Amounts withheld from salary payments will be credited to Accounts 68, 72, 73, and 76 based on the nature of the withholding. The total will be debited to Account 70, Payroll. As an illustration, assume that an enterprise makes deductions from monthly salary payments of 27,000 rubles as follows: for taxes, 12,000 rubles; for goods bought on credit, 6,200 rubles; on the basis of executive orders for benefit of third parties, 4,200 rubles; for individual insurance, 4,600 rubles. The following entry will be recorded:

Dr. Account 70 Payroll   27,000 rub.
    Cr. Account 68 Payments to State Budget   12,000 rub.
    Cr. Account 73 Claims Against Employees for
                Personal and Other Loans   6,200 rub.
    Cr. Account 76 Payments to/Claims against
                Sundry Debtors and Creditors   8,800 rub.

Subsequent payment of these amounts from the enterprise cash account will result in a credit to Account 51, Cash in Bank.

To evenly distribute vacation outlays for the year among production costs, enterprises each month reserve a specific percentage of recorded salary payments. The reserved amounts are debited to the synthetic accounts for production costs and credited to Account 89, Reserves for Future Expenses and Payments. This procedure is applied for workers whose salaries are determined using a piece-work or time-spent basis. The pay for vacations of administrative and management personnel, all of whom receive fixed salaries, is not reserved since the funding for their salary payments is determined for twelve-month periods and thus anticipates payments for vacation time. The following entry is used to record the amounts determined as reserves for vacation payments:

Dr. Account 20 Principal Work in Process
Dr. Account 23 Auxiliary Departments
Dr. Account 24 Expenses for Use and Maintenance of Equipment
Dr. Account 25 Departmental Manufacturing Overhead
Dr. Account 26 Factory Manufacturing Overhead
Dr. Account 29 Nonindustrial Facilities and Departments
      Cr. Account 89 Reserves for Future Expenses and Payments

The accounts debited are the same as for recording salary payments. The reserved amounts will be maintained in Account 89 until used for current payments. When the amount required is determined the following entry will be recorded:

Dr. Account 89 Reserves for Future Expenses and Payments
      Cr. Account 70 Payroll

The credit balance of Account 89 indicates the amount remaining for future use.
      Each month, enterprises include an amount in their production costs for the purpose of creating a special fund for workers' social security benefits. This special fund provides benefit payments to workers who are sick or partially or fully incapacitated. The amount reserved for social security benefits is calculated by applying a percentage established by the government, currently 8 percent in machine-building enterprises, to principal and supplementary salary payments for all classifications of employees. The amount reserved is charged to appropriate accounts as follows:

Dr. Account 20 Principal Work in Process
Dr. Account 23 Auxiliary Departments
Dr. Account 24 Expenses for Use and Maintenance of Equipment
Dr. Account 25 Departmental Manufacturing Overhead
Dr. Account 26 Factory Manufacturing Overhead
Dr. Account 28 Cost of Spoiled production
Dr. Account 29 Nonindustrial Facilities and Departments
Dr. Account 31 Prepaid Expenses for Future Periods
Dr. Account 43 Nonmanufacturing Expenses
Dr. Account 85 State Equity Fund
      Cr. Account 69 Insurance Premium Payments

When the amount of benefits payable to an employee is determined, the accounting department makes the following entry:

Dr. Account 69 Insurance Premium Payments
     Cr. Account 70 Payroll

The actual payment of benefits is recorded as follows:

Dr. Account 70 Payroll
     Cr. Account 50 Petty Cash or Account 51 Cash in Bank

The credit balance of Account 69, Insurance Premium Payments, indicates excess reserves that the enterprise must pay to the governmental social security agency.

14

Accounting for Production Costs

THE IMPORTANCE AND CLASSIFICATION OF ENTERPRISE PRODUCTION COSTS

In the Soviet Union great significance is attached to the product's cost to the enterprise. Government agencies responsible for the performance of industry demand that enterprises continually reduce their costs of production. Several means are employed to reduce costs: increasing labor productivity and economical use of materials, reducing or eliminating losses due to spoilage, reducing administrative and managerial costs, and promoting specialization within and cooperation among enterprises. In these efforts much importance is attributed to enterprise accounting systems and procedures. They must provide data for timely, complete, and reliable determination of unit costs and total production costs; they must permit control over utilization of materials, labor, energy, monetary, and other resources; and they must provide data for coordination of enterprise efforts to reduce production costs.

In all segments of industry in the Soviet Union there is a single methodological basis of accounting for and calculation of product cost. This circumstance makes it easier to generalize data of individual enterprises so they have significance for industry segments and the national economy. The single methodological basis also creates favorable conditions for planning and analysis of individual enterprise activity. Nevertheless, methods of accounting for product cost do vary from enterprise to enterprise. This is due to differences in enterprise size, production levels, and availability of technology, and to differences in planning methods and conditions for technical norm-setting. Regardless of differences, cost classification is critical to the determination of product cost. Certain aspects of cost classification in Soviet industry correspond with practices used in American industry; others show essential differences. At the first level of classification, costs may be grouped as follows: by source of production (from production or auxiliary departments or nonindustrial facilities and departments), by division of the enterprise (specific department), by type of product or service (product line), and by stage in the production process (activity or function being performed). The following categories are also used for classifying costs: type of labor used, relationship to the sphere of circulation, relationship to the production process, method of inclusion in the cost of production, relationship to the accounting period, relationship to the volume of production, and degree of cost complexity. Each category is explained below.

Type of Labor Used

Distinction is made between substantial labor which has already been used in the production process and live labor which will be used currently or in the future.

Relationship to the Sphere of Circulation

Distinction is made between costs incurred during the production process and costs incurred during exchange (provisioning, distribution and sale).

Relationship to the Production Process

Distinction is made between principal costs, closely related to the production process, and manufacturing overhead, which has a circumstantial relationship to the production process. Principal costs are those that are directly connected with production including those for production materials, energy, and salaries for industrial workers. Manufacturing overhead costs are those connected with production management and support. They include, for example, salaries for administrative and managerial personnel, costs incurred for maintenance of factory buildings, and amounts for amortization of plant assets. These costs are further subdivided into costs relating to specific departments and those relating to the factory as a whole.

Method of Inclusion in the Cost of Production

Distinction is made between direct and indirect costs. Direct costs are those that, on the basis of source documents, can be traced directly to a specific product or service since they were incurred as a result of production or performance. Indirect costs cannot be directly traced to a specific product or service since they were incurred in the production of all products and/or the performance of all services. The majority of such indirect costs are allocated artificially among all products and services. Some indirect costs, however, are distributed directly; those for transport within the factory, for example, are distributed in proportion to the weight of the unfinished goods transported. The government urges enterprises to reduce the portion of costs that are indirect because, no matter how indirect costs are distributed, it is impossible to completely avoid distortion of the cost of production. The division of costs as direct and indirect should not be considered the same as their classification as principal costs and manufacturing overhead since under certain conditions, principal costs are distributed indirectly.

Relationship to the Accounting Period

Distinction is made among costs of the current accounting period, costs of future accounting periods and impending costs. Costs of the current accounting period include those incurred during the current period which should be included in the cost of production for the period. Costs of future accounting periods are those incurred in the current period but subject to inclusion in the cost of products to be manufactured in subsequent accounting periods (rent payments made in advance). Impending costs are those that have not yet been incurred, but, for the purpose of correctly reflecting actual cost to the enterprise, should be included in production costs for the current accounting period (amounts reserved for worker vacations).

Relationship to the Volume of Production

In this context costs are considered variable or fixed. Variable costs are those that change when the volume of production changes. The greater the volume, the more materials used, the higher the amounts paid for salaries and the greater the amount of energy used; on the other hand, the less the volume, the less such costs are incurred. However, this dependence of variable costs on volume of production is not always proportionate: Variable costs may increase to a lesser degree than volume because, as volume increases to specific levels, favorable conditions for more efficient use of plant assets, materials, labor, and energy are created. Fixed costs are those that are not related to volume of production; included are general factory costs which do not increase with production volume. However, in certain instances fixed costs do increase when production volume increases, but, since these increases are often insignificant, fixed costs are still considered constant.

Degree of Cost Complexity

Distinction is made between elementary costs which are uniform in their economic composition and complex costs which vary in elements of their economic composition. Costs of production materials, energy, and salaries of industrial workers are elementary costs. The category of complex costs includes, for example, those for equipment maintenance which include cost elements for spare parts, fuel, and salaries of maintenance personnel, and overhead costs which include cost elements for materials, salaries, amortization, and others. Classifying costs by degree of complexity permits the summation of costs for the national economy since the system of cost classification is the same in all segments of industry. On the basis of these summaries, national planning bodies prepare estimates of future production costs, while enterprise accounting departments conduct reviews of actual production costs.

Classification by item is an additional arrangement utilized to account for production costs and for calculating unit product and total production costs. In machine-building enterprises various combinations of the following cost items are used:

1. Raw and processed materials (principal and auxiliary),
2. Reusable scrap,
3. Purchased semifinished components, accessories, and services, of cooperating enterprises,
4. The enterprise's own semifinished products,
5. Fuel used for manufacturing purposes,
6. Energy used for manufacturing purposes,
7. Purchasing and transport costs,
8. Principal salary payments for production workers,
9. Supplementary salary payments for production workers,
10. Social security reserves for production workers,
11. Costs for development of new products,
12. Costs for use of low-cost expendable items and special-purpose items,
13. Costs of equipment maintenance and use,
14. Departmental manufacturing overhead,
15. Factory manufacturing overhead,
16. Cost of spoiled production,
Total Factory Cost, Items 1 through 16;
17. Nonmanufacturing costs,
Total Cost of Production, Items 1 through 17.

Total factory cost includes all costs of production incurred by an enterprise before the product goes to the warehouse (Items 1-16). Nonmanufacturing costs (Item 17) include those connected with distribution and sale of the product. The total cost of production includes total factory cost and nonmanufacturing costs. The functions of enterprise accounting departments in controlling the cost of the product begin with accounting for production costs and end with calculation of the total cost of the finished product.

CONTROL OF PRINCIPAL PRODUCTION COSTS

The cost items included in total factory cost (Items 1-16) include two (Items 14 and 15) related to manufacturing overhead. The others are principal costs which are classified within three groups: Material (Items 1-7, 12), Labor (Items 8-10), and Complex costs (Items 11, 13, 16).

Item 1, Raw and processed materials, is the most costly production item in Soviet industrial enterprises. Source documents prepared during production are used to maintain strict control over the handling and use of materials. These documents include material cutting forms which specify the quantity of a cut material that should be used for a specific quantity of product and route forms which specify standards for use of a specific material and stay with the material through the entire production process. The cost of principal materials is written off immediately after use as part of the cost of the product for which they are used. A direct designation method of costing is normally used. In some circumstances, when it is impossible to distribute materials costs directly, they are written off indirectly to production. In these circumstances materials remain principal cost items, but at the same time acquire the characteristics of indirect costs. Any variances from standards are added to or deducted from the standard cost of the materials. Auxiliary or indirect materials are those used in production that are not considered principal materials due to their insignificant cost; they are usually accounted for in the same manner as principal materials. Usage standards for auxiliary materials may be established directly for each unit of product or indirectly using sample products. To simplify accounting, the cost of auxiliary materials is written off in proportion to established standards, the weight of reprocessed raw materials or the weight of finished products. Packaging materials issued for finished products before their being sent to the warehouse are accounted for in the same manner as principal materials. The cost of packaging used as the finished product is delivered from the warehouse to customers is accounted for among nonmanufacturing costs (Item 17).

Item 2, Reusable scrap, includes the remnants (shavings, chips, etc.) of materials used in the production process. If scrap cannot be used immediately it is returned to the warehouse where it accumulates. Scrap with value undiminished by the production process is valued using the cost of the original materials. Scrap with a reduced value and scrap that cannot be used in principal production are valued at scrap prices if reprocessing is not possible. Scrap that is distributed and sold must often go through several reprocessing steps. All costs incurred in reprocessing are recorded in Account 23, Auxiliary Departments. The cost of materials used in production is reduced by the value of reusable scrap. Scrap that is not reused, such as dried-out, pulverized, or vaporized materials, has no value and is not accounted for.

Item 3, Purchased semifinished components, accessories, and services of cooperating enterprises, includes separate parts and assemblies that are received from other enterprises and used in principal production. Their cost is written off to the appropriate units of production on the basis of initial documentation. The cost of services provided by other enterprises is also distributed directly to the appropriate units of production.

Item 4, Semifinished goods produced by the enterprise itself, includes those that have been brought to a specific stage of completion and are to be used for further manufacture or assembly of other products. The cost of the enterprise's own semifinished goods is usually written off in full as part of the cost of the products for which they are intended. In some circumstances, the cost of semifinished goods is separated by element and included in the cost of the products by element rather than as a complex cost.

Item 5, Fuel used for manufacturing purposes, is accounted for at the location of its consumption. If consumed in the production of specific products, its cost is written off directly as part of the cost of those products. The cost of fuel is written off indirectly if it is consumed during the manufacture of various products, either on the basis of the quantity of principal materials used or on the basis of units produced.

Item 6, Energy used for manufacturing purposes, may be electrical energy, steam, gas, or compressed air. The use of electrical energy is measured in kilowatts-per-hour and its cost is distributed to units produced in accordance with fixed standards. The use of other forms of energy is accounted for in a similar manner. If the energy is received from a source outside the enterprise its cost is credited to Account 60, Suppliers and Contractors Accounts Payable. The cost of energy produced by the enterprise's own auxiliary departments is credited to Account 23, Auxiliary Departments.

Item 7, Purchasing and transport costs, includes those arising in loading, unloading, and delivery of materials as well as those for maintaining purchasing agencies and warehouses near suppliers. Also included are costs of business travel to suppliers and shortages of materials during shipment resulting from natural causes. These costs are written off as part of the cost of production based on the cost of materials used.

Item 8, Principal salary payments for production workers, is for industrial workers participating directly in the production process and is usually determined on the basis of units produced. Bonuses and pay for work beyond normal conditions may also be included. Principal salary payments for production workers are distributed to production on the basis of source documents such as work orders and managers' reports. All variances from standards must be explained by accompanying documentation.

Item 9, Supplementary salary payments for production workers, includes payments primarily for vacations and other excused absences; they are written off to production in proportion to principal salary payments.

Item 10, Social security reserves, is created by including appropriate amounts in the cost of production. The amounts are determined using an established percent of principal and supplementary salary payments and are written off to production in proportion to principal salary payments. Social security reserves for industrial workers not involved in production are first charged to appropriate departmental and factory manufacturing overhead accounts.

Item 11, Costs for assimilation of new products, includes costs incurred for planning new products and developing procedures for their manufacture, installation or adjustment of related equipment, training of workers, and production of first models. It is necessary to emphasize that development of new products in the Soviet Union does not occur as frequently as in the United States; progress in innovation is very slow. Costs for assimilation of new products are considered costs of future accounting periods. They are accumulated in Account 31, Prepaid Expenses for Future Periods, and transferred each month to departmental and factory manufacturing overhead accounts.

Item 12, Costs for use of low-cost expendable items and special-purpose items, is written off as part of the cost of the products for which the items were purchased or manufactured. Costs for making tools, instruments, and accessories required to produce non-recurring special orders are charged directly to the costs of those orders when they are begun.

Item 13, Costs of equipment maintenance and use, is a complex cost item including numerous cost elements: the cost of auxiliary materials needed for equipment maintenance, principal and supplementary salary payments and reserves for special security for workers who service and operate equipment, and the cost of energy required for machine use. An analytical record of all costs of equipment maintenance and use is provided by departmental schedules. A synthetic account, Account 24, Expenses for Use and Maintenance of Equipment, is maintained to accumulate these costs. Costs recorded in this account are allocated to production using cost coefficients developed by enterprise planning departments. If mass production is mechanized or automated these costs may be allocated in proportion to industrial workers' principal salary payments.

Item 14, Departmental manufacturing overhead, and Item 15, Factory manufacturing overhead, will be described in the next section of this chapter.

Item 16, Cost of spoiled production, characterizes the quality of an enterprise's output so it is necessary to accumulate spoilage costs as a separate item. Soviet industrial products, even those that have been inspected and approved, are distinguished by their low quality; they are often unattractive and unreliable. Only absolutely worthless goods are designated as spoilage, that is, unfit for distribution and sale. These goods constitute losses that reach significant proportions in Soviet enterprises. Soviet industrial enterprises use Account 28, Cost of Spoiled Production, to control the cost of the spoilage. The cost of spoilage and costs to rework spoilage are accumulated on the debit side of Account 28 and amounts intended to reduce losses from spoilage, such as recoveries from responsible parties, are credited to the account. The debit balance of this account is transferred each month to Account 20, Principal Work in Process, as part of the cost of the product from which the spoilage evolved.

OVERHEAD AND NONMANUFACTURING COSTS

Manufacturing overhead costs are considered complex costs attributable to the support and management of the production process. They are classified as Departmental manufacturing overhead and Factory manufacturing overhead.

Item 14, Departmental manufacturing overhead, includes salary payments and social security reserves for engineering-technical, clerical, and maintenance personnel. Also included are maintenance and amortization of departmental plant assets, amortization of low-cost expendable items, costs of maintaining efficiency and safety, and losses from shortages and spoilage of materials during production and shortages in work in process discovered by inventory. Many departmental manufacturing overhead costs are fixed costs since they are not related to the volume of production, although some industrial enterprises include the cost of auxiliary materials, supplementary salary payments, and social security reserves for production workers. This practice helps to avoid extensive cost allocation since many costs are combined. Control of departmental manufacturing overhead is provided through use of Account 25, Departmental Manufacturing Overhead, which provides for recording of all relevant costs. The total accumulated on the debit side of Account 25 is allocated at the end of each month in proportion to the principal salary payments of production workers. Allocations are made to the production of appropriate departments. As a result, Account 25 is closed each month by transferring the amounts that have accumulated to Account 20, Principal Work in Process; Account 23, Auxiliary Departments; Account 28, Cost of Spoiled Production; and Account 31, Prepaid Expenses for Future Periods. Thus, Account 25 is considered a synthetic accumulation and allocation account.

Item 15, Factory manufacturing overhead, includes costs incurred for support and management of the total enterprise divided into the following cost categories: administrative and managerial costs, general operational costs, assessed fees, and nonproductive factory costs. Administrative and managerial costs include salary payments and social security reserves for administrative and managerial personnel, costs of business travel and personnel transfers, maintenance of administrative buildings, offices and vehicles, and costs incurred for office supplies and printing and postal services. General operational costs consist of those for the operation of warehouses for storage of materials and finished products, for the operation of inspection and quality control laboratories, and for the security of enterprise property. Assessed fees include such costs as taxes, customs and legal fees, charges for environmental pollution, and fees for inspection and regulation of measuring instruments. Nonproductive factory costs include losses resulting from workers' idle time due to machine breakdowns and power outages and from shortages and spoilage of materials and finished products in warehouses when the responsible party cannot be determined. Factory manufacturing overhead is applied each month to production as well as to the costs of capital construction and capital repairs. Factory manufacturing overhead is allocated in proportion to the principal salary payments of production workers. Synthetic accumulation and allocation account, Account 26, Factory Manufacturing Overhead, is assigned for recording all relevant costs. Recording in this account is carried out using a special journal which contains the classifications of costs described above. The format of the journal provides balances for each month and the year. For efficient control of factory manufacturing overhead, budgeted standards are shown in the journal to permit comparison with actual costs at any time.

Item 17, Nonmanufacturing costs, includes those for distribution and sale of products such as costs for marketing, packing, and conveyance of the finished product, and discounts to customers. In addition, this item includes costs for experimentation and research for new products and processes, contributions to the state fund for assimilation of new equipment, and costs for service under product guarantees to customers. Accounting for these costs is provided for in Account 43, Nonmanufacturing Expenses. The allocation of nonmanufacturing costs to products that have been distributed and sold is described in the following chapter.

COSTS OF PRODUCTION AND SERVICES OF AUXILIARY DEPARTMENTS

Products and services of auxiliary departments are used primarily by enterprise production departments but may also be sold or rendered to other enterprises. Large enterprises have several auxiliary departments which vary in their organization and operation and thus employ various methods of accounting for the costs of their production and services. Auxiliary department costs may be either principal or overhead costs. The cost of materials, the salary payments of industrial workers and the cost of energy consumed are the most significant principal costs; costs for maintenance of equipment and administrative and management costs constitute the significant overhead costs. Accounting for costs of auxiliary departments is performed in the same manner as for production departments, but Account 23, Auxiliary Departments, is used. This controlling account is divided into separate subsidiary accounts, each devoted to a separate auxiliary department. Each subsidiary account accumulates the costs of production and services rendered by the auxiliary department to enterprise production departments or incurred as a result of external sales. The manufacturing overhead of auxiliary departments is reflected as a separate item, being recorded directly in Account 23, or passing through Account 25, Departmental Manufacturing Overhead.

The cost of production and services of auxiliary departments may be allocated directly to the cost of principal production. Alternatively, such costs may be transferred to departmental or factory manufacturing overhead; at the end of the accounting period these costs will ultimately be allocated to the cost of principal production. These allocations require entries similar to the following:

Dr. Account 20 Principal Work in Process
Dr. Account 25 Departmental Manufacturing Overhead
Dr. Account 26 Factory Manufacturing Overhead
        Cr. Account 23 Auxiliary Departments

The costs of auxiliary departments are allocated monthly except for those of the mechanical repair and instrument manufacturing departments which represent their work in process. Production and services of auxiliary departments used within the factory are not subject to factory overhead allocations. The costs of auxiliary departments are allocated to production departments and other divisions of the enterprise on the basis of actual measurements or predetermined coefficients. If the production or services of auxiliary departments are used for capital construction or capital repair within the enterprise or sold for external use, the appropriate amount of factory manufacturing overhead is written off to these products or services. The unit cost of an auxiliary department's output is determined by dividing total departmental costs for the month by the number of units manufactured or volume of services rendered. In departments that produce diverse products the sum of costs accumulated for a specific job-order or process is divided by the units manufactured.

The auxiliary departments of an enterprise interact with one another. Thus, the mechanical repairs department uses the output (steam or water) of the steam-power department which, in turn, requires the services of the mechanical repairs department and the transportation department. This situation results in significant difficulties in determining the costs of production and services because, to determine the cost of one department, it is necessary to determine in advance the cost of production that department will incur. In such cases, the production costs of some auxiliary departments are determined using the planned cost for the current accounting period or the actual cost of such production or services for the preceding accounting period. The costs of products and services of auxiliary departments are normally entered at planned cost into the cost records of the consuming departments. The difference between planned and actual costs is entered directly into Account 20, Principal Work in Process, without distribution by product.

SYNTHETIC COST ACCOUNTING TRANSACTIONS

Account 20, Principal Work in Process, and Account 23, Auxiliary Departments, are used to accumulate the costs related to production. Account 20 absorbs costs related to principal production and Account 23 the costs of production and services of auxiliary departments. Three other accounts are used to accumulate costs which are subject to future allocation: Account 24, Expenses for Use and Maintenance of Equipment; Account 25, Departmental Manufacturing Overhead; and Account 26, Factory Manufacturing Overhead. These accounts are designated for the recording, classification and allocation of costs for production management and support and factory administration.

Account 20, Principal Work in Process, is used to accumulate all production costs by element. Direct costs for items such as materials, energy, and salary payments of production workers are entered directly while the majority of indirect costs, for maintenance of equipment and departmental and factory manufacturing overhead, are first recorded in appropriate accumulation and allocation accounts. At the end of each month they will be transferred to Accounts 20, Principal Work in Process, and 23, Auxiliary Departments. The synthetic Account 23, Auxiliary Departments, is designated to accumulate both direct and indirect costs related to the production and services of these departments. At the end of each month appropriate amounts are transferred to Account 20, Principal Work in Process, and Account 03, Capital Repairs. The costs of production and services of auxiliary departments designated for external use and sold outside the enterprise will be transferred to Account 46, Sales. Costs not transferred represent the production and services of auxiliary departments consumed by the departments themselves.

Table 14.1 presents a series of cost accounting transactions and entries to illustrate the general use of synthetic accounts for recording production costs in a Soviet industrial enterprise. The accounting transactions and entries presented in Table 14.1 may also be illustrated by a schema, Figure 14.1, which provides a complete visual portrayal of the correspondence of accounts. Analytical accounting for production costs is extremely labor-intensive and is performed in records whose format permits detailing of costs by element, item, and job order or stage in the production process.

Table 14.1
Basic Cost Accounting Transactions and Entries

	Transaction Number and Content	Corresponding Accounts Dr.	Cr.
	Issuance of materials:		05
1	for principal production	20	
2	for production needs of auxiliary departments	23	
3	for routine repair and maintenance of equipment	24	
4	for maintenance of departmental locations	25	
5	for maintenance of administrative offices	26	
6	for carrying out labor safety measures	25	
7	for developing new products	31	
	Usage of fuel:		06
8	for principal production	20	
9	for production needs of auxiliary departments	23	
10	for operation of equipment	24	
11	for heating departmental locations	25	
12	for heating administrative offices	26	
13	Accepting bill from external organization for repairs or other services	31	60
	Determination of amounts of principal and supplementary salary payments:		70
14	for workers in principal production	20	
15	for workers in auxiliary departments	23	
16	for workers servicing equipment	24	
17	for supervisory personnel of departments	25	
18	for factory administrative personnel	26	
19	for workers developing new products	31	
	Reserving of amounts for social security:		69
20	for workers in principal production	20	
21	for workers in auxiliary departments	23	
22	for workers servicing equipment	24	
23	for supervisory personnel of departments	25	
24	for factory administrative personnel	26	
25	for workers developing new products	31	

Table 14.1 continued

Transaction Number and Content	Corresponding Accounts Dr.	Cr.
Reserving of amounts for vacations:		89
26 for workers in principal production	20	
27 for workers in auxiliary departments	23	
28 for workers servicing equipment	24	
29 for supervisory personnel of departments	25	
30 for factory administrative personnel	26	
31 for workers developing new products	31	
Amortization of plant assets:		86
32 for machinery and equipment in production departments	24	
33 for plant assets in general departmental use	25	
34 for plant assets in general factory/administrative use	26	
Amortization of low-cost expendable items:		13
35 for items used in principal production	25	
36 for items used by auxiliary departments	23	
37 Amortization of low-cost expendable items of special designation	20	13
38 Allocation of costs of equipment use and maintenance to production	20	24
Allocation of departmental manufacturing overhead:		25
39 to principal production	20	
40 to production and services of auxiliary departments	23	
Allocation of factory manufacturing overhead:		26
41 to principal production	20	
42 to production and services of auxiliary departments	23	
43 Allocation of costs of auxiliary production and services to principal production	20	23
Transfer of reusable scrap discovered in production departments to warehouse:		20
44 as production materials	05	
45 as fuel	05	
Discovery of spoiled production:		
46 spoilage separated from good production	28	20
47 spoilage reusable as material	05	28
48 cost of spoilage withheld from responsible parties	70	28
49 losses from spoilage added to principal production	20	28
50 Transfer of finished goods to warehouse	40	20

Figure 14.1
General Schema of Cost Account Correspondence[a]

#05 Production Materials
06 Fuel and Combustible Materials
13 Amortization of Low Cost Expendable Items
50 Petty Cash
60 Suppliers and Contractors Accounts Payable
69 Insurance Premium Payments
70 Payroll
86 Amortization Fund
89 Reserves for Future Expenses and Payments

Dr.	Cr.

#20 Principal Work in Process

Dr.	Cr.

#40 Finished Goods

Dr.	Cr.

◄——————————(1, 8, 14, 20, 26, 37)——————————►

#24 Expenses for Use and Maintenance of Equipment
25 Departmental Manufacturing Overhead
26 Factory Manufacturing Overhead
31 Prepaid Expenses for Future Periods

Dr.	Cr.

◄——————(50)——————►

◄——————(38, 39, 41)——————►

#23 Auxiliary Departments

Dr.	Cr.

#28 Cost of Spoiled Production

Dr.	Cr.

◄——(3,4,5,6,7)——►
◄——(10,11,12)——►
◄——(13)——►
◄——(16,17,18,19)——►   ◄——(40,42)——►   ◄——(43)——►   ◄——(46)——►
◄——(22,23,24,25)——►   (49)
◄——(28,29,30,31)——►
◄——(32,33,34)——►
◄——(35)——►

◄——(2,9,15,21,27,36)——►

(44,45)

(47,48)

[a] The numbers in parentheses correspond to transaction numbers from Table 14.1

15

Inventorying of Production and Cost Determination

INVENTORYING AND VALUATION OF UNFINISHED PRODUCTION

Each manufacturing process calls for the completion of a number of production activities. The product that is not processed through all stages is regarded as unfinished work in process. Two types of production are considered unfinished in the machine-building industry: products whose processing has not been completed in a specific production department and products whose processing within a department has been completed but which must be sent to another department for further processing or assembly. Other products considered unfinished are those lacking accessories or which have not been subject to tests required before they can be considered marketable. Unfinished production does not include materials or purchased semifinished products located in production departments for which processing has not yet begun. Reparable spoilage that will be used in the manufacture of other products is considered unfinished production.

Inventorying is the means of determining the existence and extent of unfinished production and spoilage that remains at each processing stage. Inventorying also allows verification of quantities and production costs recorded in the accounting records and assists in determination of the cost of the finished product. In taking inventory the actual quantity of unfinished items is counted and recorded on special inventory lists; the last stage the product has passed through must be indicated. Surpluses and shortages are discovered, often resulting from extra requirements being written into manufacturing orders, from concealment of spoilage and from loss of component parts. Such deviations must be shown in the accounting records. The process of inventorying is usually conducted by enterprise inventory committees. These groups examine differences between actual data and accounting records, determine their causes, and suggest measures to control unreconciled differences in the future. With approval of the government, shortages are written off to Account 84, Shortages and Losses from Damages; the amounts are then transferred to Account 25, Departmental Manufacturing Overhead. Surpluses are debited to appropriate manufacturing cost accounts with the corresponding credit to Account 25, Departmental Manufacturing Overhead.

Unfinished production is usually valued at actual cost to the enterprise but machine-building enterprises that use standard costs may use them as a basis for valuation. Standards for materials, salaries, and other direct costs incurred for the actual stages of completion during inventorying are used. A simplified approach requires that the actual quantity of items in process be multiplied by 50 percent of standard labor cost. This is based on the assumption that the average percentage of completion for unfinished products is 50 percent. The standard cost of materials is then added and departmental and factory manufacturing overhead are allocated in proportion to the principal salary payments of production workers; however, the amounts allocated will not exceed amounts budgeted.

CALCULATING THE COST OF PRODUCTION

Cost calculation is the determination of the manufactured value of the product in monetary expression; it is inseparably linked to accounting. Specific accounting procedures are followed for calculation of the costs of manufactured products; these cost calculations are also needed to meet additional accounting, budgeting, and statistical requirements. Soviet practice distinguishes calculation of planned, budgeted, and actual cost. Planned cost, which represents the anticipated cost of a product or group of homogeneous products, is determined before the beginning of an accounting period or when a production department receives a current order to produce a product not previously planned. The planned cost is based on the expected costs of material, labor, energy, and strictly limited cost allocations for manufacturing overhead. The objective of planned cost calculations is to lower the actual costs incurred during production; planned cost is the desired level of production cost. The planned cost is the level of cost which should be the average incurred during the planning period, either one year or one quarter.

Budgeted cost represents the base of calculation when standard costs are used. Budgeting commences shortly before the production process begins and is based on the standards in effect at that time. Usually the standards set for budget calculations are very tight and require supreme efforts from workers and managers combined with a minimum of expenditures. In the course of a month standards may be changed many times. Any change of standards must be immediately reflected in budgeted cost calculations and the new standard used when making comparisons with actual cost. Planned cost calculations are the first step toward the calculation of budgeted costs. Budgeted costs always reflect less tolerance and more tension than planned costs. Actual cost calculation is performed at the end of an accounting period (a month, a quarter, or a year) or after completion of a specific job-order. This calculation is prepared on the basis of accounting data which include the accumulation of actual production costs by element.   The planned and budgeted cost calculations in Soviet industrial enterprises are usually prepared by enterprise planning departments, while actual cost calculations and their consequent analyses are performed by enterprise accounting departments.

Depending on the complexity of the production process employed and the quantities and characteristics of the goods produced, Soviet industrial enterprises use three cost accumulation/calculation methods: the simple method, the job-order method, and the process costing method. Each may be employed using actual or standard costs. The simple costing method in the machine-building industry is applied primarily to the production and services of auxiliary departments. It is used for basic manufactured homogeneous output when neither unfinished work in process nor incomplete production is involved; the simple method is used particularly to calculate the cost of electrical energy, steam, gas, and compressed air. The actual cost of a unit of energy is calculated by dividing the total cost accumulated by the units of output.

The job-order method of cost accumulation and calculation is employed by enterprises manufacturing a single unique product or small series of identical products. With this method all costs related to specific job-orders are accumulated in separate records (job cost sheets). When complex products requiring use of lengthy and complicated manufacturing processes are produced, the general job-order is subdivided by component parts or individual machine assembly groups; each then becomes a single job-order. This enables the enterprise to determine the actual cost of an individual component at any stage of production without waiting for all work to be completed. When the job-order method is used, the cost of production represented by a job-order can be calculated only after all production for the order, including inspection and testing, has been completed. At that time all costs will be accumulated by element in appropriate records. Materials and unfinished goods that remain after a job-order is completed must be returned to the warehouse for future use. The cost of these items will be deducted from Account 20, Principal Work in Process, thus reducing the cost of the completed job.

To determine the cost of production at the end of the month during which a job-order was completed, all direct and indirect costs incurred are accumulated and reduced by the value of returns mentioned previously but also by the value of reusable scrap and wasted materials. If only one unit of product was ordered and manufactured, its cost will be the total of all costs incurred minus the total of all deductions. If the order called for the manufacture of several units, the cost of one unit is determined by dividing total net costs by the number of units produced. If a finished product is sent to a customer or to the warehouse in parts before completion of the job and, consequently, before the actual cost is determined, the planned cost of this portion of the job will be removed from the Account 20, Principal Work in Process. When a large quantity of complex products is manufactured in one job-order, many materials are needed and their cost constitutes a substantial part of the total cost. Therefore, in calculating the cost of the job-order, the cost of materials may be divided by major groups to indicate the quantity and cost of the most valuable materials used.

The process method of cost accumulation and calculation is employed for mass production manufacturing when a homogeneous principal material is used and the product passes through several steps which gradually transform the raw material into a finished product. This transformation which includes a number of work operations occurs in processing stages; the work operations are performed in the production departments of the enterprise. As material passes through the processing stages it may first become a semifinished product, then a completed unit. The essence of process costing is the inclusion of all costs incurred during the first processing stage as part of the cost of the second processing stage. The costs of the second processing stage, which include those of the first stage, will be transferred and added to the cost of the third processing stage and so on. This process of consecutive additions continues until the product is completed. In machine-building enterprises process costing is used in the production of castings; in enterprises producing chemicals, foodstuffs, and textiles this method predominates. Thus, process costing may also be used when several products are manufactured from a homogeneous principal material. In determining the costs incurred at each processing stage, it is important to realize that the cost of unfinished production remaining from the previous accounting period (work in process inventory) can vary significantly. Therefore, for accurate cost calculations, the costs of the beginning and ending work in process inventories should be determined by element. This can be accomplished by using the equivalent units calculation as it is performed in American industry. If the cost of the remaining work in process is stable or insignificant, then all costs of unfinished production at one processing stage will be included in the cost of production of the next stage and the work in process inventory will be ignored.

The three methods of cost accumulation and calculation (simple, job-order, and process costing) and any combination of them can be used with actual costs or standard costs. The significance of using actual costs is that the final (actual) cost of production as well as variances from planned cost are determinable only at the end of the accounting period. Thus, the results may be available not only after the product has been manufactured but often after it has been distributed and sold. It is obvious that the results of a comparison between actual cost and planned cost are useless because it is too late to influence the cost of the product; opportunities to reduce actual cost no longer exist. It is more important to discover variances from planned cost during the production process. The use of standard costs, or the normative method as it is referred to in Soviet accounting, accomplishes this.

USE OF STANDARD COSTS

Standard costs can be combined with the job-order costing method and the process costing method; these combined methods of cost accumulation and calculation are referred to as Job-order standard cost accounting and Process standard cost accounting. Standard costs may also be used alone as well. When the actual cost of production is calculated by cost element and cost item, variances are determined for specific job-orders or processes. When standard costs are used in this manner, it is necessary to predetermine the standards for each element and item of production cost. The standards that form the basis of standard costs are systematically corrected as manufacturing techniques and processes are improved. Recorded changes in the standards, to permit accounting simplification, are made only at the beginning of the month.

When standard costs are used, the actual cost of production may be determined on the basis of standard costs predetermined by cost element considering the following:

A. The beginning inventory of work in process at standard cost,
B. Changes in original standards carried over with the beginning inventory of work in process,
C. Costs incurred during the current accounting period at standard,
D. Changes in current standards for the costs incurred,
E. Variances of actual costs from standards,
F. The ending inventory of work in process at new standard cost.

The actual cost of production is the algebraic sum of these six indicators. The actual cost of one unit of production when standard costs are used can be calculated by formula using the indicators A through F, with N equal to the number of good units manufactured, savings indicated by a minus sign $(-)$, and overexpenditures by a plus sign $(+)$: $(A \pm B + C \pm D \pm E - F) \div N$. The standard cost of production by cost element and cost item is determined by multiplying the number of units produced by the standard costs per unit in effect during the current month. The actual cost of a unit is its standard cost adjusted by variances revealed by job order or process. If the standard and actual costs of a product are known by cost element and cost item, it is possible to calculate a variance index which simplifies all additional cost calculations. If, for example, the standard cost of materials for a product is predetermined as 3,200 rubles and the actual cost is 3,197 rubles, the variance index for materials will be 0.999 ($3,197 \div 3,200$). The actual cost of a unit of product is calculated by multiplying the standard cost of its cost elements or cost items by the variance indexes as shown in Table 15.1.

Table 15.1
Calculation of Actual Cost of Rear Automobile Chassis

Elements of Cost	Standard Cost in Rubles	Variance Index	Actual Cost in Rubles
Materials	7.40	0.999	7.39
Purchased Assembly Parts	10.00	0.952	9.52
Salaries (principal)			
Chassis Department	1.60	1.002	1.60
Previous Departments	1.30	0.920	1.20
Costs of Equipment Maintenance	3.20	1.000	3.20
Departmental Manufacturing Overhead			
Chassis Department	2.90	1.000	2.90
Previous Departments	4.80	1.005	4.82
Depreciation of Tools and Instruments			
Chassis Department	0.40	1.047	0.42
Previous Departments	0.70	1.008	0.71
Totals	32.30		31.76

Soviet enterprises must include in their annual accounting report a schedule providing full disclosure of all costs of production and an attachment indicating the costs of the most important and expensive products. These statements present planned and actual costs of resources consumed and related variances, explanations of variances, and measures taken to correct unfavorable variances. The official instructions for planning and accounting and for calculation of production cost in the machine-building industry distinguish some divisions, such as aircraft production and shipbuilding,[1] where cost accounting procedures differ from those previously presented.

16

Accounting for the
Finished Product

NATURE, VALUATION, AND STORAGE

The circulation of economic resources in an enterprise is completed by the sale of the finished product. Product distribution and sale present few problems since consumers normally accept most goods because of chronic shortages of almost all products. Soviet enterprises are also free of problems of pricing and competition: Prices are set by the government and there is virtually no competition among enterprises. Accounting for the finished product must reflect output, storage, shipment, distribution, sales, consumer payments, and sales results. All products manufactured by Soviet enterprises are considered state property. Those products distributed and sold externally for money are called commodities. Also considered state property are partially completed components, services performed for outside customers, and the products and services of the enterprise used for its own capital construction and repair activities. A finished product is one that has passed through all stages of processing and testing, meeting appropriate standards, and has been accepted by an inspection controller.

The valuation of finished products used in accounting records, known as the accounting price, may be determined using one of three alternative bases: actual factory costs, average quarterly or annual planned factory costs, or the selling prices of the enterprise. The first method of determining the accounting price is based on actual factory cost. This method is the easiest to apply but its use is restricted to enterprises whose range of products is very limited. This restriction is necessary since production, distribution and sale of the finished product can take place daily while calculation of its cost to the enterprise occurs only at the end of the month. Consequently, when this method is used, a value is placed on a product previously produced, distributed, and sold. Such delays significantly reduce the usefulness of accounting information, thus reducing the possibility of influencing the process of distribution and sale.

The second method of pricing for finished products utilizes average quarterly or annual planned factory costs. Variances are segregated and subsequently written off to the cost of goods sold. Using this method, variances between actual cost and planned cost are calculated and transferred among accounts as production, distribution, and sale take place. To accomplish this the average percentage of variance between actual and planned cost is determined by using the following formula:

$$\text{Average Percentage of Variance} = \frac{\begin{array}{l}\text{Variance between actual and planned cost at beginning of the month}\end{array} + \begin{array}{l}\text{Variance between actual and planned cost for the current month}\end{array}}{\begin{array}{l}\text{Finished goods inventory at beginning of the month at planned cost}\end{array} + \begin{array}{l}\text{Output of finished goods for the current month at planned cost}\end{array}} \times 100$$

The percentage determined is used to calculate the amount of the adjustment to the cost of goods sold. If the amount represents a cost overage (an unfavorable variance) the entry in the corresponding accounts appears in dark ink and is added in determining account balances. If the amount represents a saving (a favorable variance) the entry is recorded in red ink and is deducted. The third method of pricing utilizes the selling price charged by the enterprise to its customers as the accounting price. The variances between actual cost and the enterprise's selling price are calculated and recorded in the same manner as those mentioned above for the second method of pricing.

Finished products are shipped to enterprise warehouses with prenumbered delivery invoices prepared by the production departments that issued the products. Each invoice includes the date, the name of the product, its inventory number, and its accounting price. Enterprises manufacturing complex and costly products assign each component an individual serial number that is shown in a special column of the delivery invoice. The serial number also appears in the accounting records and on the technical documentation for each component. Detailed information for finished products is maintained in accounting records common to enterprise warehouses and accounting departments. The quantitative recordkeeping for finished products in the warehouse is conducted in the same manner as the recordkeeping for materials. Release of finished products from the warehouse for shipment is reflected in both the warehouse quantitative records, and those of the accounting department, which also reflect the monetary effects of the completed transaction.

SHIPMENT, DISTRIBUTION, AND SALE

Account 40, Finished Goods, is used to account for finished products that have been received from enterprise production departments and are available for sale. The debit side of Account 40 also indicates the value of services generated by the enterprise. The credit side of the account indicates the value of products sold and services rendered. The value of goods shipped by the enterprise is recorded in Account 45, Goods Shipped and Services Rendered, which functions as a suspense account since finished products are not considered sold until payment is received. This account is also used for recording the value of products and services used for capital construction and repair of the enterprise's own facilities. The following entry is recorded to indicate shipments:

Dr. Account 45 Goods Shipped and Services Rendered
    Cr. Account 40 Finished Goods

At the moment of shipment the actual cost of the product has usually not been determined; the entry will be recorded at the accounting price. When the actual cost of the goods or services is determined, its variance from planned cost or selling price will be entered in Accounts 40 and 45 in black (overage) or red (saving). Thus, the actual cost of goods shipped will appear independently for the first time in Account 45. In the course of delivery of finished products, the enterprise incurs costs for packing and conveyance; these costs may be for materials used or they may be direct cash outlays. These costs are always anticipated in drafting enterprise sales contracts and are recorded on the debit side of Account 43, Nonmanufacturing Expenses. Costs that, according to the terms of the sales contract, will be reimbursed to the enterprise by the purchaser are transferred directly to the debit side of Account 45, Goods Shipped and Services Rendered.

Shipped goods whose specifications do not match those indicated by the terms of the sales contract may be rejected by the customer. In such cases the customer, having refused to accept the goods, must store them and record the transaction by a single entry in Off-Balance-Sheet Account 002, Merchandise and Goods in Custody, and also inform the selling enterprise in writing of the decision not to accept the goods. Customers accepting goods shipped must pay for them within the established period. Only when the seller receives payment for goods shipped is the sale considered completed. American companies using the accrual basis of accounting will normally recognize sales revenue upon shipment (revenue principle). Completed sales are recorded by Soviet enterprises in Account 46, Sales, which is used to accumulate both the actual cost of goods sold and the selling price. Thus, Account 46 shows the results of sale (income or loss). In addition to the distribution and sale of finished products, Account 46 is used to record sales of products manufactured from scrap and sales of products from the enterprise's own agricultural facilities.

An illustration of the accounting procedures for distribution and sale of finished products is now presented. Assume that the production departments of a manufacturing enterprise produce and send to the warehouse finished products with a planned cost of 60,000 rubles; subsequent calculation discloses that the actual cost is 58,800 rubles. Thus, the variance between actual and planned cost is 1,200 rubles or a saving of 2 percent. The following day, finished products costing 40,000 rubles (planned cost) are sold to a customer in another city; the actual cost of products sold is 39,200 rubles (40,000 × .98). Using its own trucks, the enterprise spends 450 rubles to transport the goods to the railroad station and load them into a freight car. In addition, the enterprise pays 1,600 rubles for rail freight on behalf of the customer. Ten days later the enterprise receives from its customer 23,800 rubles, of which 23,000 rubles represent half the selling price and 800 rubles partial reimbursement of the rail freight charges. Only those products valued at 20,000 rubles using planned cost, but with an actual cost of 19,600 rubles (20,000 × .98), are considered sold. The preceding transactions are the basis for the following entries:

1. To record transfer of finished products to the warehouse at planned cost:
      Dr. Account 40 Finished Goods   60,000 rub.
            Cr. Account 20 Principal Work in Process   60,000 rub.
2. To record shipment of the product to the customer at planned cost:
      Dr. Account 45 Goods Shipped and Services
                            Rendered 40,000 rub.
            Cr. Account 40 Finished Goods   40,000 rub.
3. To record transport and loading costs incurred:
      Dr. Account 43 Nonmanufacturing Expenses   450 rub.
            Cr. Account 23 Auxiliary Departments   450 rub.

The rail freight charge of 1,600 rubles may be paid by the enterprise with limited or unlimited checks received from the State Bank of the USSR. If paid with an unlimited check, the bank has effectively granted a short-term loan for expenses connected with the finished product. Debiting Account 45 indicates that the freight paid by the enterprise is to be reimbursed by the customer with payment for the goods.

4. To record the check for rail freight charges paid by the bank:
      Dr. Account 45 Goods Shipped and Services
                            Rendered 1,600 rub.
            Cr. Account 90 Short-term Bank Loans
                            Payable   1,600 rub.
5. To record receipt of payment from the customer at selling price including reimbursement for the applicable rail freight charges:

      Dr. Account 51 Cash in Bank   23,800 rub.
            Cr. Account 46 Sales   23,000 rub.
            Cr. Account 45 Goods Shipped and
                  Services Rendered   800 rub.

6. To record transfer of the planned cost of products sold remaining in
   Account 45:
      Dr. Account 46 Sales   20,000 rub.
            Cr. Account 45 Goods Shipped and
                  Services Rendered   20,000 rub.

Since the debit balances of Accounts 40, Finished Goods; 45, Goods Shipped and Services Rendered; and 46, Sales, still include the planned cost of the products sold, these accounts must be adjusted by the favorable variance of 2 percent to permit comparison of selling price with actual product cost. This is accomplished by recording in red ink three simultaneous entries for 400 rubles (20,000 × .02):

7a. Dr. Account 40 Finished Goods   400 rub.
         Cr. Account 20 Principal Work in Process   400 rub.
  b. Dr. Account 45 Goods Shipped and Services Rendered 400 rub.
        Cr. Account 40 Finished Goods   400 rub.
  c. Dr. Account 46 Sales   400 rub.
        Cr. Account 45 Goods Shipped and Services
                      Rendered   400 rub.

The cost of the products sold debited to Account 46, Sales, will be incomplete unless related nonmanufacturing costs are transferred to this account; the costs transferred are the amounts corresponding to the proportion of finished products considered sold. Since only half of the finished products, valued at 20,000 rubles, have been sold, transport and loading costs of 225 rubles will be transferred to Account 46 by the following entry:

8. Dr. Account 46 Sales   225 rub.
        Cr. Account 43 Nonmanufacturing Expenses   225 rub.

The remaining nonmanufacturing costs not written off by the end of the month are grouped with the sum of the goods shipped and are reflected on the balance sheet with that item.

      The government levies a sales tax on many products as a means of centralizing a portion of the revenues generated by each enterprise. The sales tax requires a payment to the State Budget according to established rates. If a tax of 1,850 rubles is levied on the products sold it is necessary to record the debt with the following entry:

9. Dr. Account 46 Sales   1,850 rub.
        Cr. Account 68 Payments to State Budget   1,850 rub.

Payment will be reflected by the following entry:

Dr. Account 68 Payments to State Budget   1,850 rub.
        Cr. Account 51 Cash in Bank   1,850 rub.

  To determine the results of product sales, it is necessary to compare the full cost of products sold, accumulated on the debit side of Account 46, with the revenue from sales credited to the same account. The difference between the total debit and credit entries in Account 46 represents the income or loss from sales transactions. Realized income is transferred to Account 80, Income and Losses, as follows:

10. Dr. Account 46 Sales   1,325 rub.
        Cr. Account 80 Income and Losses   1,325 rub.

  The effects of the preceding sales transactions and the relationship among accounts can be illustrated by a schema, Figure 16.1. Entries analogous to the above will be recorded for transactions reflecting use of products and services for the enterprise's own capital construction and repair activities.

Figure 16.1

General Schema of Sales Transactions and Related Accounts[a]

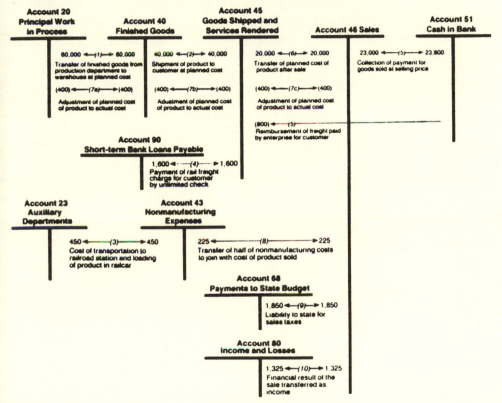

Account 20
Principal Work
in Process

60,000 ◄—(1)—► 60,000
Transfer of finished goods from
production department to
warehouse at planned cost

(400) ◄——(7a)——► (400)
Adjustment of planned cost
of product to actual cost

Account 40
Finished Goods

40,000 ◄—(2)—► 40,000
Shipment of product to
customer at planned cost

(400) ◄——(7b)——► (400)
Adjustment of planned cost
of product to actual cost

Account 45
Goods Shipped and
Services Rendered

20,000 ◄—(6)—► 20,000
Transfer of planned cost of
product after sale

(400) ◄——(7c)——► (400)
Adjustment of planned cost
of product to actual cost

(800) ◄——(5)
Reimbursement of freight paid
by enterprise for customer

Account 46 Sales

23,000 ◄—(5)—► 23,800
Collection of payment for
goods sold at selling price

Account 51
Cash in Bank

Account 90
Short-term Bank Loans Payable

1,600 ◄——(4)—— ► 1,600
Payment of rail freight
charge for customer
by unlimited check

Account 23
Auxiliary
Departments

450 ◄——(3)——► 450
Cost of transportation to
railroad station and loading
of product in railcar

Account 43
Nonmanufacturing
Expenses

225 ◄——————(8)——————► 225
Transfer of half of nonmanufacturing costs
to join with cost of product sold

Account 68
Payments to State Budget

1,850 ◄——(9)—► 1,850
Liability to state for
sales taxes

Account 80
Income and Losses

1,325 ◄——(10)—► 1,325
Financial result of the
sale transferred as
income

[a]The numbers in parentheses correspond to transactions from pages 136-38.

17

Accounting for Cash and Credit Transactions

THE USE AND CONTROL OF ENTERPRISE CASH

The economic activity of any industrial enterprise causes mutual payment relationships which arise between the enterprise and other enterprises, nonindustrial organizations, and individual persons. When one enterprise obtains material resources or services from other enterprises or organizations, the payments are made without cash by transferring amounts from the account of the payer to the account of the payee. This form of mutual payment is widely used in the Soviet Union; it is called a noncash payment. Actual cash payments are made through enterprise cashier's offices only for salaries, pensions, compensation for temporary disability, and as small advances to accountable employees.

The state apportions to each self-supporting enterprise a limited amount of cash resources sufficient for normal operation. However, in certain cases an enterprise may temporarily receive additional funds from the State Bank of the USSR which offers short-term credit for special purposes such as formation of seasonal reserves of materials or fuel or for projects related to productivity improvements. Accounting for enterprise cash resources and indebtedness requires timely and substantiated recording which ensures the continuous availability of information about the flow and balance of cash resources, the enterprises's financial standing in relation to the State Budget, the status of its payment relationships with others, and its credit obligations to the State Bank.

The cash resources of an enterprise are held in a bank account at the State Bank; only a strictly limited amount of funds may be held in the enterprise cashier's office. A bank account is opened for each enterprise that is established by the state and provided with circulating assets and required to file its own independent balance sheet and accounting reports. The bank account is used for recording various cash transactions related to purchases of materials, sales of finished goods, and payments and collections for services. The account is also used for recording numerous other cash-related transactions: receipts of funds from the State Budget to replenish circulating assets, reimbursements to the enterprise for losses predetermined by its technical-industrial-financial plan, payments to the State Budget for sales taxes and allocations from the enterprise's net income, receipts from and transfers to government agencies to accomplish redistribution of circulating assets among enterprises, and payments and receipts related to credit obtained from the bank. Each of these transactions is carried out by the State Bank as a noncash payment. The bank will, as necessary, issue a certain amount of cash to each enterprise for specific payments. All payments from an enterprise's bank account are satisfied by the bank only within the limit of cash resources available in the account. Personal and business checks like those commonly used in the United States do not exist in the Soviet Union. Special checks are used only to make payments to transport and communication organizations.

To maintain control over cash resources, enterprise accounting departments use Account 51, Cash in Bank. Each entry in this account is recorded on the basis of bank statements and verifying documents received daily. Each bank statement indicates the starting balance of the enterprise's account for the day, amounts added to and paid from the account, and the balance of cash at the end of the day. Each day the accounting department compares the statement with its own records to verify its accuracy. When an error is detected the enterprise must inform the bank in writing and record the amount in Account 63, Claims against Responsible Persons, or Account 76, Payments to/Claims against Sundry Debtors and Creditors. The accounts corresponding with Account 51, Cash in Bank, are shown in Figure 17.1.

The enterprise cashier's office is where small amounts of cash are received, held, and disbursed. The amount on hand, usually between 300 and 500 rubles, is limited to that sufficient for immediate or emergency needs. The limit is established by the State Bank of the USSR for each enterprise. For salary payments which are always paid in cash, and payments for business travel, each enterprise requests from the State Bank the required amount of cash which is deposited in a safe deposit box in the cashier's office. Inflows of cash to the cashier's office may arise from collections from customers, usually in amounts less than 100 rubles; all amounts collected must be deposited in the bank the same day. All cash received by the enterprise must go to the cashier's office and only the cashier can make cash payments. The cashier must maintain a standardized cash book for receipts and disbursements and calculate the petty cash balance each day. Accounting for petty cash is provided for using Account 50, Petty Cash. Correspondence of other accounts with Account 50 is shown in Appendix B, the Schema of General Ledger Account Correspondence.

Specified amounts of enterprise cash may be held by employees authorized to disburse cash for expenses that cannot be paid through the bank or by the cashier's office. Employees spend this cash when the enterprise must make small retail purchases or buy train tickets for employee business trips. To

Figure 17.1
Accounts Corresponding with Account 51, Cash in Bank

Debits (increases)	Credits (decreases)
Credited to Account 50, Petty Cash, cash received from the enterprise cashier's office.	Debited to Account 50, Petty Cash, cash sent to the enterprise cashier's office.
Credited to Account 46, Sales, cash collected from product sales.	Debited to Account 60, Suppliers and Contractors Accounts Payable, payments to suppliers and contractors.
Credited to Account 76, Payments to/Claims against Sundry Debtors and Creditors, collection of accounts receivable.	Debited to Account 68, Payments to State Budget, sales taxes paid to the state.
Credited to Account 85, State Equity Fund, amounts received from the state to replenish circulating assets.	Debited to Account 81, Distribution of Net Income, the portion of enterprise net income paid to the state.
Credited to Account 90, Short-term Bank Loans Payable, short-term loans received from the State Bank.	Debited to Account 90, Short-term Bank Loans Payable, amounts paid to the State Bank to satisfy short-term loans.
In appropriate circumstances debits to this account may also correspond with credits to Accounts 45, 54, 55, 56, 60, 61, 63, 71, 72, 73.	In appropriate circumstances credits to this account may also correspond with debits to Accounts 25, 26, 29, 43, 54, 55, 56, 61, 63, 69.

provide for such expenses, the enterprise advances cash in limited amounts to certain accountable employees. Control of cash issued to these persons is provided by use of synthetic account 71, Accountable Cash on Hand, and a subsidiary account for each accountable employee. Cash disbursed is reflected on the debit side of Account 71 while the credit side indicates payments by the accountable employee and returns of unused advances to the cashier. Complete correspondence of all accounts with Account 71, Accountable Cash on Hand, is shown by Appendix B, the Schema of General Ledger Account

Correspondence.   All entries in Account 71 must be supported by documentation verified by the enterprise accounting department and confirmed by the enterprise's director or his first assistant.

SETTLING ACCOUNTS WITH CUSTOMERS AND SUPPLIERS

As previously mentioned, industrial enterprises enter into financial relationships that begin with shipments of goods or rendering of services and end with payments for those goods and services. These relationships are started and terminated each business day. Depending on the nature of the transactions, a variety of payment methods is used to settle customer and supplier accounts. The acceptance method of payment is the most widespread; it is advantageous to the customer because it gives him the opportunity to inspect the goods before payment. After a shipment of goods, the supplier instructs his bank branch to settle with the customer at the customer's location. The supplier provides the bank with the appropriate documents and request for payment which are forwarded to the customer. The sales transaction is considered complete only if the supplier receives payment from the customer.

The letter-of-credit method of payment provides for payment between customer and supplier at the supplier's location. If this method is used the more secure party in the transaction is the supplier. This method is used primarily by suppliers of timber and oil and also with customers who do not always make timely payments; it is employed as well for single shipments to distant cities or when the customer has been placed by the State Bank on a special regimen of credits and payments. This method of payment requires the customer to instruct his bank branch to present a letter of credit insuring that the bank will transfer to the supplier's bank branch the specified amount within the time allowed. After requesting a letter of credit from the bank branch, the customer records the following entry for the appropriate amount:

Dr. Account 55 Other Accounts in Bank
    Cr. Account 51 Cash in Bank

A debit is also recorded in Subaccount 55-2, Letters of Credit. After the supplier ships the product or renders the service, the supplier's bank branch processes the letter of credit and the specified amount, with a corresponding credit to Subaccount 55-2, passes to the supplier's account.

Planned installment payments are commonly used when there are continuing regular deliveries of goods by the supplier to the customer. Under this method the customer, daily or every few days, pays the supplier an amount stipulated by agreement. Every five, ten, or fifteen days payments are brought up-to-date: the customer pays the supplier any unpaid amounts or the supplier returns any overpayments. All payments are authorized by special form letters and are executed through the State Bank. Accounting for transactions using planned installment payments will be reflected in Account 61, Installment Payables and Receivables.

Payments by bank check are used to settle obligations for transportation and communication services. A check gives the bank authority to pay the specified amount from the customer's account to the holder of the check who may be a supplier who has prepaid shipping charges for the customer. Industrial enterprises use two forms of payment checks: those from limited checkbooks and those from unlimited checkbooks. The difference between the two forms is clearly indicated when the bank issues the checkbook. A payment ceiling or upper limit is specified on the cover of the limited checkbook while no such limit is imposed on unlimited checks. When issuing limited checkbooks, the bank withdraws the amount of the established limit from the enterprise's account and the enterprise records the following entry:

Dr. Account 55 Other Accounts in Bank
    Cr. Account 51 Cash in Bank

The customer, by settling with suppliers for services received by giving them limited checks, enables the supplier to receive payment through the bank. The customer records the amounts paid by limited checks with a variation of the following entry determined by the nature of the expenditures:

Dr. Account 05 Production Materials
Dr. Account 43 Nonmanufacturing Expenses
Dr. Account 45 Goods Shipped and Services Rendered
Dr. Account 60 Suppliers and Contractors Accounts Payable
    Cr. Account 55 Other Accounts in Bank

The unused portion of the amount specified as the checkbook limit will be returned by the bank to the customer's account to be reflected by the following entry:

Dr. Account 51 Cash in Bank
    Cr. Account 55 Other Accounts in Bank

Payments made with unlimited checks are recorded differently. Checks received and presented by the supplier and paid by the customer's bank branch automatically involve the granting of a short-term loan.

ADDITIONAL PAYMENT RELATIONSHIPS

In addition to transactions among themselves, many Soviet industrial enterprises develop payment relationships within the enterprise, with ministries and other administrative agencies of the government, and with the State Budget. Settlement of obligations between an enterprise and its controlling ministry or an agency thereof may arise from redistribution of circulating assets and net income. The enterprise uses Account 77, Mutual Payments and Claims for Intrasystem Redistribution of Circulating Assets and Income, to record these transactions. The enterprise records cash resources transferred to higher administrative agencies as debits to Account 77 and cash resources received as credits. At the administrative agency level the entries are the mirror-image of the enterprise's entries: debits for cash resources transferred to the enterprise and credits for cash resources received. At the end of the year the balance of Account 77 is transferred to Account 85, State Equity Fund. Thus, cash resources received from administrative agencies during the year became part of the State Equity Fund allocated to the enterprise; cash resources transferred decrease State Equity Fund allocations to the enterprise.

Sometimes production departments of large enterprises are granted limited autonomy, the primary purpose being to increase the responsibilities of the department's management. These departments remain part of the enterprise, but they receive their own accountability and must prepare a balance sheet for each accounting period. In this situation payment relationships arise between the enterprise and its independent departments. The enterprise and its independent departments use Account 79, Interdepartmental Payments and Claims, to account for these transactions.

Each Soviet enterprise and administrative agency must settle its payment obligations to the State Budget including those for sales and withheld income taxes and those for unclaimed funds for which statutory holding periods have expired. The various payments to the State Budget are accounted for using Account 68, Payments to State Budget. Account 68 has several subaccounts assigned to specific types of payments: 68-1, Sales Taxes; 68-2, Fees for Plant and Circulating Assets; 68-3, Fixed Rent Payments; 68-4, Balance of Net Income; 68-5, Deductions from Net Income; 68-6, Income Taxes Withheld from Salaries and Wages Paid to Employees; 68-7, Other Payments.

SHORT-TERM AND LONG-TERM BORROWING

The State Bank grants enterprises short- and long-term loans designated for specific purposes and having definite conditions for repayment. In granting loans, the State Bank considers the nature of the enterprise's activity and the circumstances that have caused the need for additional funds. All loans provided are limited to an amount determined in relation to the enterprise's technical-industrial-financial plan. Loans received are recorded by each enterprise in Account 51, Cash in Bank. Planned short-term loans may be granted when an enterprise must purchase materials beyond planned limits or when surpluses of unfinished or completed goods result from seasonal variations. Loans for the time necessary to collect customer accounts receivable are provided when a supplier presents documents attesting to the shipment of goods or performance of services. The amount of the loan is usually sufficient to cover the planned cost or wholesale price, not the selling price, of the goods shipped or services rendered. Loans for temporary discretionary needs are considered privileged since they are granted only to enterprises that successfully fulfill their annual plans. This credit is granted for purposes of reward or incentive for terms up to ninety days. Enterprises may use these funds for other than normal operations: to conduct additional research, to introduce new products, or to increase productivity. Long-term loans for periods of one to six years are granted to enterprises to introduce new technology and to improve or expand the production of consumer goods. It is anticipated that enterprises will repay these loans from savings obtained by reducing product costs or from additional income earned by increasing sales.

Transactions between enterprises and the State Bank for short-term loans are accounted for using Account 90, Short-term Bank Loans Payable. This synthetic account is subdivided into several detailed analytical accounts according to the purpose of the loan. When a loan is granted and received into the enterprise's bank account, it is reflected in the enterprise's accounting records by the following entry:

Dr. Account 51 Cash in Bank
    Cr. Account 90 Short-term Bank Loans Payable

If the loan is used to satisfy directly a debt or payment due, it is recorded by a debit to Account 60, Suppliers and Contractors Accounts Payable. Satisfaction of the loan by the enterprise will be recorded by a reversal of the first entry. Long-term loan transactions are recorded in Account 92, Long-term Bank Loans Payable. The credit side of this account indicates loans received from the bank and the debit side the satisfaction of loans by the enterprise.

18

Accounting for Funds, Financial Results, and Price Changes

THE STATE EQUITY FUND

The funds described in this chapter are considered the most important sources of economic resources for industrial enterprises in the Soviet Union. These funds include the State Equity Fund, the Funds for Economic Stimulation and Special Purposes, and the Amortization Fund for plant assets, which was described in Chapter 11. When the state establishes a self-supporting enterprise, it allocates a specific amount of economic resources to the enterprise; this constitutes the State Equity Fund. The amount of the fund also indicates the obligation of the enterprise to the state for these resources. Since the economic resources of an enterprise include plant assets and circulating assets, the State Equity Fund of each enterprise consists of two parts: the first assigned to plant assets and the second assigned to circulating assets. The former has a value equal to the residual cost (book value) of the plant assets, the latter part, equal to the remainder of the fund, represents the value assigned to the circulating assets. If the historical cost of an enterprise's assets is 140,000 rubles, the accumulated depreciation 50,000 rubles, and the total of the State Equity Fund 162,000 rubles, the part of the fund subsidizing plant assets will be 90,000 rubles (140,000 − 50,000) and that subsidizing circulating assets will be 72,000 rubles (162,000 − 90,000).

The State Equity Fund does not remain constant. It increases upon receipt from the state of additional subsidies for replenishment of circulating assets or for reimbursement for planned losses; it decreases upon transfer to the state of circulating asset surpluses. Redistribution of circulating assets among enterprises, executed by order of higher administrative bodies, also changes the balance of the State Equity Fund. The balance may be increased if a portion of the net income remaining at the disposal of the enterprise is added. In addition, all changes in the volume or valuation of plant assets influence the State Equity Fund by increasing or decreasing it. All Soviet enterprises use Account 85, State Equity Fund, to account for transactions affecting the fund. This account is considered a passive account on the balance sheet. It belongs to the group of accounts reflecting the origins of an enterprise's economic resources. Transactions that increase the fund balance are recorded on the credit side of Account 85; those that decrease it are recorded on the debit side. Synthetic account 85, State Equity Fund, is divided into two subaccounts: 85-1, State Equity Fund and 85-2, Subsidies from State Budget. Amounts actually received from the State Budget to replenish circulating assets and for reimbursement of planned losses are added to the State Equity Fund at the end of the year by an internal entry within Account 85. The entry is as follows:

Dr. Subaccount 85-2 Subsidies from State Budget
    Cr. Subaccount 85-1 State Equity Fund

Accounting for transactions affecting the State Equity Fund is carried out in such a way that their effects on the part designated for plant assets and the part designated for circulating assets are subdivided within the same account as shown in Figure 18.1.

FINANCIAL RESULTS AND DISTRIBUTION OF NET INCOME

In addition to the various funds, the net income of an industrial enterprise is an important source of its economic resources. Enterprise net income is derived primarily from profitable sale of its products. When the selling prices of the products sold exceed their full actual cost the enterprise usually generates net income. In some cases, however, the result of sales may be negative and the enterprise suffers losses. The profitability of a Soviet enterprise is more an ideological than an economic factor. The government tolerates the existence of unprofitable enterprises, such as those producing bread and socialist publications, for social and political purposes. An enterprise may earn income or suffer losses not directly related to the sale of its products. These non-sale-related items include losses from bad debt write-offs and natural disasters, income or losses from operation of enterprise housing and personal service facilities, and penalties related to violations of contractual obligations. Interest paid on bank loans is also considered a non-sale-related reduction in enterprise net income. The balance of income or loss represents the final financial result of the enterprise's economic activity. Under normal conditions the non-sale-related items represent an insignificant portion of an enterprise's net income or loss.

All Soviet enterprises use active-passive account 80, Income and Losses, to account for financial results. The positive or negative results of product sales are transferred to this account monthly from Account 46, Sales. Income and losses from non-sale-related transactions are not included in sales revenue

Figure 18.1
Effects of Various Transactions on Account 85, State Equity Fund[a]

Debits (decreases)	Credits (increases)
Designated for plant assets	Designated for plant assets
Disposal of plant assets, corresponds with credit to Account 01, Plant Assets.	Acquisition of plant assets, corresponds with debit to Account 01, Plant Assets.
Recording of amortization, corresponds with credit to Account 02, Accumulated Depreciation.	Reduction in amortization due to disposal or capital repair, corresponds with debit to Account 02, Accumulated Depreciation.
Designated for circulating assets	Designated for circulating assets
Use of materials, fuel and spare parts; payment of expenses and salaries; and social security reserves related to disposal of plant assets, corresponds with credits to Accounts 05, Production Materials; 06, Fuel and Combustible Materials; 08, Spare Parts for Plant Assets; 50, Petty Cash; 51, Cash in Bank; 60, Suppliers and Contractors Accounts Payable; 70, Payroll; 69, Insurance Premium Payments.	Returns of materials, fuel and spare parts remaining from disposal of plant assets, corresponds with debits to Accounts 05, Production Materials; 06, Fuel and Combustible Materials; 08, Spare Parts for Plant Assets.
Losses resulting from disposal of plant assets, corresponds with credit to Account 80, Income and Losses.	Replenishment of fund by addition of state-authorized subsidies, corresponds with debit to Account 77, Mutual Payments and Claims for Intrasystem Redistribution of Circulating Assets and Income.
	Replenishment of fund by the portion of net income designated at year-end, corresponds with debit to Account 80, Income and Losses.

[a]Certain events (recording of amortization) may affect only the part designated for plant assets, only the part designated for circulating assets (distribution of net income), or both parts (disposal of a plant asset).

or the cost of production and are entered directly into Account 80; losses are reflected on the debit side and income on the credit side. The balance of the account indicates the final financial result of the enterprise's economic activity. The financial result is positive if the credit amounts exceed the debit amounts; it is negative if the debit amounts are higher. Losses from the year's activity will cause reductions in the State Equity Fund.

Distribution of the net income is the final result of an enterprise's annual economic activity. The results of the distribution will be shown in the accounting records for the following year. The order of priority for income distribution is regulated by the state. Certain payments have precedence including payments to the State Budget, assessments for plant and circulating asset use, assessments based on net income, and interest on bank loans. Amounts are then apportioned for the formation of funds for economic stimulation and special purposes. The remainder of the net income is directed toward satisfaction of bank loans granted for capital investments, increasing the enterprise's own resources, and reimbursement of losses from operation of housing and personal service facilities. Payments to the State Budget are based on the planned level of net income and that generated above the planned level. The amounts are determined using the income reflected in the balance sheet and a percentage established by the government for each segment of industry. Payments for use of plant and circulating assets are based on a percentage of the value of those assets used in production. When determining asset value, certain assets are excluded: plant assets acquired using production improvement funds or unpaid bank loans, spare plant assets, and inventories above normal operating levels not funded by bank loans. Special taxes based on net income are paid only by large enterprises with substantial profits owing to especially favorable operating conditions.

Entries for payments to the State Budget are recorded in synthetic account 68, Payments to State Budget, which has several subsidiary accounts relating to the nature of the payments. Enterprises make payments to the State Budget several times during the year but the amounts are not recorded as distributions of net income until the end of the year. This deferral permits analysis of the enterprise's actual financial results at that time. Current payments to the State Budget are recorded by the following entry:

Dr. Account 81 Distribution of Net Income
    Cr. Account 51 Cash in Bank

At the end of the year after examination of the annual accounting report, the total payable to the State Budget will be determined and the following entry recorded:

Dr. Account 80 Income and Losses
    Cr. Account 68 Payments to State Budget

An adjustment for amounts previously transferred to the state will be recorded with the following entry:

Dr. Account 68 Payments to State Budget
    Cr. Account 81 Distribution of Net Income

The remaining debit or credit balance in Account 68, indicating a refund due or an additional amount payable, will be written off by one of the following entries. If a debit balance indicating that current payments exceed actual enterprise net income:

Dr. Account 51 Cash in Bank
    Cr. Account 68 Payments to State Budget

If a credit balance indicating that current payments are less than actual enterprise net income:

Dr. Account 68 Payments to State Budget
    Cr. Account 51 Cash in Bank

Other payments and distributions of net income are recorded on the debit side of Account 80, Income and Losses. Corresponding credits are recorded in several other accounts: Account 51, Cash in Bank (for interest payments on bank loans); Account 76, Payments to/Claims against Sundry Debtors and Creditors (for penalties for violation of delivery contracts); and Account 85, State Equity Fund (for the portion of enterprise net income retained).

FUNDS FOR ECONOMIC STIMULATION AND SPECIAL PURPOSES

A small portion of the net income generated by Soviet industrial enterprises is usually allotted to create funds for economic stimulation and special purposes. Soviet planning and accounting procedures provide for several funds, each having a specific purpose. The common feature of all funds is their formation by deductions from enterprise net income. Thus, the amount allocated depends on the amount of net income and the volume of goods manufactured and sold. Also important are political and economic factors considered in the examination of the enterprise's annual accounting report. The eleven funds for economic stimulation and special purposes differ from one another in essential ways and will be described briefly. The fund for stimulating incentives (1) is created for granting bonuses to industrial workers and engineering-technical and clerical personnel for conscientious performance and achievement of work quotas established in the enterprise's technical-industrial-financial plan. The fund for cultural and personal service facilities and housing construction (2) is used for improvement of cultural, medical, and personal services for employees, for housing construction, and for the construction and maintenance of child care centers. The fund for improvement of productivity (3) is created by deductions from net income but also through amortization of plant assets and gains from sale of surplus plant assets.

The fund for bonuses for achievements in self-improvement (4) is created from net income generated above the planned level or from savings due to expenditures below planned levels of product cost for enterprises expected to operate at a loss. This fund supports a form of socialist competition sponsored by the Communist Party. Individuals and teams compete within enterprises and with other enterprises for bonuses awarded for success in fulfilling commitments to improve productivity, modify personal behavior, and enhance ideological convictions. The fund for promotion of consumer goods manufacturing (5) is created from net income generated from sale of consumer goods. This fund is formed only in enterprises with departments specializing in the production of consumer goods from waste and scrap material remaining from production departments manufacturing other products. Resources of this fund are used for expansion of consumer goods production departments, improvement in the quality of consumer goods, bonuses to workers involved in production of consumer goods, and for improvement and repair of workers' housing. The fund for integration of new equipment (6) is created by authority of responsible ministries from amounts paid by machine-building, metal processing, and other enterprises; these payments are recorded by the enterprise in Account 43, Nonmanufacturing Expenses. This centralized fund is used to cover enterprise costs connected with incorporation and use of new machinery and processes. The fund for bonuses for creation and introduction of new equipment and technology (7) is created by indirectly including special charges in the total cost of production; the amount is recorded in Account 43, Nonmanufacturing Expenses. The resources of this fund are used for granting bonuses to those who have contributed substantially toward creating and introducing new equipment and technology within the enterprise. Evaluation is based on examination of the enterprise's annual activity and economic efficiency.

The fund for bonuses for producing export goods (8) is created only by enterprises that manufacture goods for export. This fund is created by including special charges in wholesale prices before adding sales taxes. This fund is used for granting individual bonuses to industrial workers, managers, and engineering-technical and clerical personnel who participate directly in production, packaging, shipping, and preparing documents for exported goods. The fund for bonuses for collecting and shipping scrap metals (9) is created from revenue received from the sale of scrap metals. This fund is used for granting bonuses to workers involved in collecting, storing, and shipping these materials. The fund for bonuses for saving fuel and electrical and steam energy (10) is created from savings generated by economical use of fuel and energy.

The resources of this fund are used for granting bonuses to those who show the best results of conservation efforts. The fund for stimulation of cultural and personal activities (11) is created from income generated from sale of products intended for cultural and personal use (artistic and musical works, barbering tools, etc.).

All funds are created to stimulate workers to improve their performance in implementing the goals of the government. The amounts funded and paid are small, but considering the modest salaries of Soviet workers, bonuses paid by enterprises to their workers are highly coveted. Accounting for funds of economic stimulation and special purposes requires use of two accounts: Account 87, Funds for Economic Stimulation, and Account 88, Funds for Special Purposes. Each of these accounts is subdivided into subsidiary accounts dedicated to each specific fund. During the year when the enterprise makes allocations to the funds, they are recorded using the following entry:

Dr. Account 81 Distribution of Net Income
    Cr. Account 87 Funds for Economic Stimulation
    Cr. Account 88 Funds for Special Purposes

The exceptions are the fund for integration of new equipment and the fund for bonuses for creation and introduction of new equipment and technology which are created by charges to nonmanufacturing expenses. After the enterprise's annual accounting report has been reviewed, the allocations to the funds will be transferred as reductions of net income as follows:

Dr. Account 80 Income and Losses
    Cr. Account 81 Distribution of Net Income

In addition to the funds for economic stimulation and special purposes, Soviet enterprises may utilize certain additional resources obtained from the state. An enterprise, for example, may receive the funding to establish and operate a social club. Such subsidies may be used only for the purposes for which they are designated. These funds are accounted for using Account 96, Special Purpose Financing/Revenue from Special Sources.

CHANGES IN WHOLESALE PRICES

Changes in wholesale prices and transportation charges have significant influence on the enterprise's cost of production, revenue, net income, and its mutual payment relationship with the State Budget. Wholesale prices in the Soviet Union are set by the government. Changes in wholesale prices are effected for three reasons: to conform to changes in the cost structure of an enterprise, to eliminate the unprofitableness of a specific enterprise or an entire segment of industry, and to influence retail prices. Changes in wholesale prices occur infrequently, once every three to ten years, and depending on the circumstances, prices may be increased or reduced.

Accounting procedures for changes in wholesale prices depend on the relevant circumstances. If new wholesale prices for all industrial products are introduced at the same time, and the enterprise technical-industrial-financial plans relating to income, circulating resources, and payment relations with the state change in a corresponding manner, the results of wholesale price changes are accounted for using Account 14, Reappraisal of Nonplant Assets. When wholesale prices are reduced, the amount is debited to Account 14 in correspondence with credits to the appropriate asset accounts (Accounts 05, 06, 08, 12, 20, etc.). When wholesale prices increase, the amount is credited to Account 14 in correspondence with debits to the appropriate asset accounts. Later the amounts charged to Account 14 will be transferred to Account 85, State Equity Fund, which indicates the obligations of the enterprise to the state.

If the change in wholesale prices occurs during the year and has not been taken into account in enterprise financial plans, enterprises that distribute and sell their products at increased wholesale prices will earn additional income, whereas enterprises that purchase these goods will incur additional costs beyond their control. To eliminate these imbalances, the additional income of the selling enterprises is transferred to the purchasing enterprises to cover their losses. This transfer is accomplished using a special fund created by the State Committee for Prices of the Council of Ministers. The fund's resources are provided by the State Budget and will be used to cover enterprise losses resulting from changes in wholesale prices. The additional income of other enterprises, resulting from advantageous changes in wholesale prices, will be used for replenishment of the fund. The adjustment of enterprise income levels is accomplished through Account 78, Intrasystem Payments and Claims from Current Transactions, and Account 14, Reappraisal of Nonplant Assets.

19

Reporting Enterprise Financial Position and Operations

PREPARATION OF ENTERPRISE ACCOUNTING REPORTS

The results of the economic activity of Soviet enterprises is summarized periodically by compiling and classifying enterprise accounting data using a special system of state-prescribed forms. The complete set of forms including addenda and explanations is referred to as the enterprise accounting report. The primary purpose of the accounting report is to present summarized economic information for critical analysis of the enterprise's past activity, for drawing up plans for future activity, for elimination of deficiencies, and for consolidation of results. The use of a standardized, single set of forms is an important distinction of Soviet enterprise financial statements. This simplifies the consolidation of information for segments of industry, branches of the economy, and the total national economy. The Ministry of Finance and the Central Statistical Administration of the Council of Ministers of the USSR define the composition and contents of accounting reports and the dates and periods for their submission. All Soviet enterprises prepare accounting reports on a monthly, quarterly, or annual basis as required. Interim monthly and quarterly reports include condensed statements and contain limited general information while the annual report is more comprehensive: it contains the greatest number of forms and the most detailed information. The annual report more completely describes the fulfillment of yearly plan guidelines for the enterprise and its financial position at the end of the year. All enterprises report on a calendar year basis. Before compiling the annual accounting report, all Soviet enterprises complete appropriate preliminary work. This begins with the reviewing of data in the accounting records; all discrepancies located are corrected. Then a complete inventorying of all assets is undertaken; deviations from accounting records must be adjusted within ten days by appropriate adjusting entries.

Asset deficiencies within the limits allowed by established norms are written off as expenses by order of the director of the enterprise. Shortages and losses due to spoilage that are beyond established norms are written off as amounts to be collected from those personally responsible. When shortages or losses are the result of malfeasance, the director of the enterprise is obliged to bring the matter before a judicial investigative body and initiate a criminal and/or civil suit not later than five days after the shortage or loss is discovered. If direct responsibility cannot be determined the related amounts are written off as expenses. The amount of any asset overage will be used to reduce the manufacturing overhead of the enterprise. Subsequently, the enterprise will attempt to determine the causes of the surpluses and those responsible for them. Offsetting deficiencies with surpluses is permitted only if certain conditions exist: The deficiencies and surpluses must arise in the same period, the same person must be responsible for them, and the deficient and surplus goods or materials must be identical. When shortages and losses are offset and such costs exceed surpluses, the difference must be recorded as amounts to be collected from those responsible. Surpluses and deficiencies in plant assets are recorded in Account 01, Plant Assets, Account 02, Accumulated Depreciation, and Account 85, State Equity Fund. Cash overages are considered state property and must be deposited in the local bank branch within three days for transfer to the State Budget. Amounts not claimed by creditors after expiration of the established credit period are also transferred to the State Budget. Amounts not collected by the enterprise from debtors before expiration of the credit period are written off as losses.

Before compilation of interim and annual accounting reports necessary adjusting and closing entries must be recorded. Certain adjusting entries, as illustrated in Figures 14.1 and 16.1, affect Accounts 24, Expenses for Use and Maintenance of Equipment; 25, Departmental Manufacturing Overhead; 26, Factory Manufacturing Overhead; 43, Nonmanufacturing Expenses; 46, Sales; and 80, Income and Losses. Expenses for the use and maintenance of equipment and departmental and factory manufacturing overhead are transferred to the principal work in process account which absorbs all manufacturing costs. The closing entry will be as follows:

Dr. Account 20 Principal Work in Process
        Cr. Account 24 Expenses for Use and Maintenance of Equipment
        Cr. Account 25 Departmental Manufacturing Overhead
        Cr. Account 26 Factory Manufacturing Overhead

Expenses accumulated on the debit of Account 43, Nonmanufacturing Expenses, are transferred to Account 46, Sales:

Dr. Account 46 Sales
        Cr. Account 43 Nonmanufacturing Expenses

Sales results recorded in Account 46 are thus offset and the net amount is transferred to Account 80, Income and Losses. If the result is positive, income from sales will be transferred by a credit to Account 80; if the result is negative the loss will be transferred as a debit.

The enterprise accounting department must also record adjusting entries necessary to distribute expenses among accounting periods, specifically in Account 31, Prepaid Expenses for Future Periods, Account 69, Insurance Premium Payments, and Account 89, Reserves for Future Expenses and Payments. The final step is the closing of the active and passive balance sheet accounts. Total increases and decreases of assets or sources thereof are calculated for each account. The ending balance is then determined and transferred to the opposite side of the same account to prove the accuracy of the posting process. All preparatory procedures are mandatory and must be completed on a timely basis.

STRUCTURE OF THE ANNUAL ACCOUNTING REPORT

The annual accounting report of a Soviet enterprise includes operative management summaries, statistical information, and the accounting statements themselves. The most important components of the report, its principal forms and appendices, will be described briefly. Form 1, The Balance Sheet for Principal Activity, presents in the active (assets) section the enterprise's existing economic resources; the passive (liabilities) section reflects the origins of those resources. Both asset and liability items are grouped in sections with their values expressed in rubles for the beginning and end of the year, similar to a comparative balance sheet in the United States. A condensed balance sheet for a Soviet industrial enterprise was previously presented in Chapter 10 as Figure 10.1. The balance sheet reflects the composition, amount, source, and disposition of the enterprise's economic resources and as such is used as the primary basis for analysis of its financial condition. The enterprise and the government can monitor the use of the enterprise's resources, the enterprise's solvency, the condition of its accounts receivable and payable, as well as its use of bank loans. Analysis of the balance sheet permits comparison of the results of the enterprise's activity for the current year or period with that of previous periods. In addition to comparisons, balance sheet data are used to calculate the turnover of assets and their sources of formation and changes in the composition of assets and their sources.

Once a month, accounting reports, which always include a balance sheet, are sent by all enterprises to the accounting departments of appropriate administrative agencies. These agencies, and the ministries to which they are responsible, audit and analyze enterprise reports and balance sheets prior to consolidating the information into one or several additional consolidated balance sheets for further analysis as a summary of the activities of the respective agencies and ministries. The Central Statistical Administration of the Council of Ministers ultimately receives all accounting reports and balance sheets. A series of additional forms and appendices supplement and explain specific balance sheet items. Together they provide a complete and more detailed picture of the financial position of the enterprise. Appendix 3 to the Balance Sheet describes the enterprise's capital construction expenditures and the related funding sources shown in Section D of the balance sheet. This information is recorded by enterprise accounting departments separately from data for the enterprise's principal operational activities. Appendix 4 discloses the results of reappraisal of assets for the current year as required by directives received from the government.

Form 2, Amendments to the Balance Sheet, explains the amount presented as Withdrawn assets in Section A of the balance sheet. Disclosed are the details of payments to the State Budget and any losses from cancelled or postponed orders. Form 3, Changes in the State Equity Fund, contains information about changes and their causes in the composition of the State Equity Fund for the current year for both plant and circulating assets. It also contains an explanation of the net income allocation for the preceding year and indicates the portion of enterprise net income allocated to the fund. Form 4, Statement of Personnel Training, discloses the enterprise's expenses for personnel training and for programs designed by the enterprise to raise the qualifications of workers, engineers, and technical personnel. Form 5, Cost of Production Statement, presents the cost of production by elements. It excludes intrafactory costs, those incurred for finished products and semifinished goods and tools manufactured by the enterprise for its own needs. All complex costs such as manufacturing overhead are analyzed and classified by element: materials, fuel, energy, amortization of plant assets, salary payments, social security reserves, etc. Data from this statement are used to study costs according to their economic composition.

Form 6, Cost of Commodity Production, consists of five parts: (1) Cost of all commodities and comparable commodity products[1] produced in the current and previous years; (2) Achievement of plans for reducing the cost of commodity production and expenditures per ruble of sales revenue collected; (3) Changes and components of expenditures per ruble of revenue from sale of commodity products at established wholesale prices; (4) Unit costs of the most important kinds of products; (5) Losses from spoilage and waste. The ratio of production cost per ruble of sales revenue for commodities (the cost to the manufacturer to earn a ruble) is considered especially important in segments of Soviet industry producing a high proportion of different products from year to year. Costs for these products cannot be evaluated by comparison. The cost and profitability of the most important products are shown in special appendices attached to Form 6. This information is usually obtained from analytical accounting records.

Form 7, Expenses for Services and Management, contains a disclosure of government-approved enterprise cost levels for use and maintenance of equipment, departmental and factory manufacturing overhead, and administrative and management expenses. Form 8, Statement on Fulfillment of the Plan for Production, presents data on enterprise production volume including a listing of the most important products produced during the current period. Less important products are listed in total. Form 9, Statement of Fulfillment of the Plan for Labor, provides disclosures in several sections: (1) Number of personnel employed and the funding for salary payments; (2) Accumulation of the fund for stimulating incentives; (3) Composition of the salary fund for production workers; (4) Other payments, excluding bonuses, to industrial and clerical workers not considered salary payments; (5) Number of production workers including the number hired and dismissed; (6) Changes in number of engineering and technical personnel; (7) Efficiencies in the use of labor.

Form 10, Changes in Financing and Special Funds, indicates financing received through the State Budget and other sources and from funds established for special purposes. Form 11, Statement of Status of Plant Assets and Changes in Amortization Fund, provides disclosures in four sections: (1) Availability and movement of plant assets; (2) Disposition and amortization of plant assets; (3) Changes in the amortization fund; (4) Repair of plant assets. Form 12, Sale of Finished Products, presents the most important data on enterprise economic activity. Form 12 reflects actual and budgeted manufacturing costs for goods sold, nonmanufacturing costs, sales taxes, revenue collected from sales of the product, and the final result of sales (net income or loss). Form 20, Net Income and Losses, reflects the sources and disposition of enterprise income and losses; the final result of this statement also appears on the balance sheet. The annual accounting report also includes a statement, Form 22, Summary of Principal Indicators, that presents the most important information from other parts of the report to provide a concise format for review of an enterprise's economic activity by managers and officials at higher levels.

In addition to the statements described above, the annual accounting report may include the following if appropriate: (1) Statement of Housing and Community Services; (2) Statement of Maintenance of Child Care Centers and Nursery Schools; (3) Statement of Shortages, Theft and Spoilage of Commodities, Materials, and Other Resources; (4) Statement of Fulfillment of the Plan for Research; (5) Statement of Composition and Use of Energy and Electric-Generating Equipment; (6) Statement of Availability of Storage Terminals for Oil and Petroleum Products. The annual accounting report is accompanied by a comprehensive explanatory letter prepared by the enterprise accounting department and signed by both the director and controller of the enterprise. The letter should objectively analyze the results of efforts toward fulfillment of the enterprise's operational plan by review of the fundamental indicators of economic activity. Suggestions for improvement must also be included. The explanatory letter also presents the results of inventorying: the shortages discovered, incidents of waste or theft that have occurred, and the measures taken to ensure recovery or future prevention of such shortages.

The directives of the Ministry of Finance and the Central Statistical Administration govern the composition of annual accounting reports. Standard forms for all documents with related instructions are published and distributed annually, several months before enterprises begin their preparation. Thus, in Soviet enterprises standardization of accounting reports, as well as the principles and procedures used in their preparation, is the norm. These requirements facilitate the consolidation of information and simplify the training of Soviet accountants and bookkeepers. Such rigid uniformity is possible only within socialist countries with highly centralized economies. However, limited standardization, especially within and among governmental agencies and large national and multinational corporations, is also possible in countries with decentralized economies.

REPORT SUBMISSION, REVIEW, AND AFFIRMATION

Annual accounting reports are submitted by each enterprise no later than January 25 of the year following that under review. They are submitted to the responsible administrative agency of the appropriate ministry, the local branch of the State Bank, and the regional office of the Central Statistical Administration. Accounting divisions of the administrative agency are responsible for the review. Accounting reports are examined for the presence of all necessary forms, the correctness with which they have been completed, and the coordination of economic indicators in corresponding statements. The accounting manual published each year by the government illustrates the relationship among the various indicators. For example, "amount on line 87 of Form 1 must be equal to the amount of line 36 of Form 20." Any differences must be explained. Similar conformities are checked for hundreds of indicators; corrections are made if necessary.

After preliminary examination of the report, a date for the official hearing of the report is established. Invitations for the hearing are sent to the director of the enterprise, its controller, the enterprise's Communist Party representative, and also to the enterprise's bank branch and the regional office of the Central Statistical Administration. During the hearing the report is discussed by the director of the enterprise, the controller, and the government official who has analyzed the report. Special attention is directed to the following areas: fulfillment of the enterprise's plan for production and sales; the profitability of the enterprise and each of its departments; the enterprise's cost of production and efforts to reduce it; the financial condition of the enterprise, its solvency, and its punctuality in making payments; the incidence of losses and theft and exposure of those responsible. After discussion of the report, allocation of the enterprise's net income is determined. The corresponding entries will be recorded in the accounting records the following year. The report examination and hearing will be described in a memorandum released by the administrative agency to the enterprise. The memorandum usually contains recognition or criticism of enterprise management for the results achieved. The memorandum also includes proposals for measures to eliminate the deficiencies of the enterprise and sustain its accomplishments.

20

Economic Analysis as a Means of Control

GENERAL CHARACTERISTICS OF ECONOMIC ANALYSIS

Economic analysis of a socialist enterprise's activity is the logical conclusion of the accounting process. Economic information is collected, processed, and reported in records and statements so that it may be subjected to economic analysis. By means of such analysis, the achievement of the enterprise's operational plan, information about the use of its assets and reserves, and factors influencing the enterprise's operations are studied and summarized. Analysis enables the enterprise to develop future plans which include efforts directed toward increasing efficiency. The productive and economic activity of the enterprise is a complex and many-sided process; it includes financing, production and sale of products, and use of technology and material resources. The productive and economic activity of the enterprise has two aspects, technical and economic. Technical and natural sciences (physics, chemistry, etc.) study technical methods and technology. Economic sciences study the economic phenomena of productive and economic activity and the economic relationships of people in the production process. Economic analysis examines economic phenomena in relation to technology and the organization of production. The productive and economic activity of an industrial enterprise is thus the object of research of a group of closely related economic sciences. Included within this group are the economics of labor and industry, planning and organization of production, enterprise financing, accounting and statistics, and, finally, economic analysis.

The basis of economic sciences in the Soviet Union has been Marxist-Leninist political economics, which studies all economic phenomena from the viewpoint of the unquestionable superiority of the socialist economy over the capitalist. Marxist-Leninist political economics recognizes only those economic phenomena that shed a favorable light on its theories. Thus, all inadequacies discovered in the course of analysis are never acknowledged as imperfections of the socialist economic system, but are always attributed to the errors and misunderstandings of individuals or small groups. Despite this limitation, the theory and practice of economic analysis in the Soviet Union over the decades of its existence has provided specific methodologies worthy of attention and study. In the following account, the theory and practice of economic analysis is presented in the manner characteristic of Soviet economic sciences. Economic analysis as a science may be divided into the following subdivisions of knowledge: (1) the theory of economic analysis which provides a description of its subject, goal, objects and objectives, activities and methodolgy; (2) economic analysis of the productive and economic activity of the enterprise by means of which specific elements of the enterprise's activity are reviewed and compared; (3) economic analysis of the activity of related enterprises (grouped by product line, sales territory, etc.) and segments of industry, the results of which enable the development and effectiveness of entire segments of industry or similar organizations to be evaluated.

Economic analysis of enterprise productive and economic activity may be classified by purpose. Operational (immediate) analysis of economic events is performed as financing, production, and sales transactions occur. Timely information is needed since operational management of the enterprise is reviewed on a daily basis. Using the data of operational analysis, an evaluation of current operations is performed and decisions on future activities are made. Operational analysis is an essential element of planning. It is performed by technical specialists, department heads, and accounting department personnel. Subsequent analysis is the review of completed enterprise activity for a month, a quarter, or a year. Information received as the result of this analysis becomes the preliminary data of future planning for the enterprise. Prospective analysis is required for periods longer than one year. It may be complex in character or focused on one aspect of an enterprise's operation. The goal of prospective analysis is to prepare data for determining the extent and prospects of the enterprise's long-term development and that of its divisions, and to determine broad economic policy for the next several years. Prospective analysis is usually performed within the enterprise in its economics laboratory by economists and production managers, and externally by members of scientific and research institutes for segments of industry. Economic analysis of the activities of related enterprises and segments of industry includes summary analysis and comparative analysis. Summary analysis is conducted to generate information necessary for centralized control of related enterprises responsible to various administrative agencies. Comparative (interfactory) analysis studies differences in the performance levels of specific enterprises with the intention of discovering opportunities for increasing the effectiveness of other enterprises and segments of industry. Suggestions for cooperation among enterprises is also an important consideration in comparative analysis.

The objects of economic analysis are the fundamental indicators of enterprise economic activity as presented in its operational plan. Analysis of the process of plan achievement requires determination and use of specific evaluative indices. These indices, among many, include volume of output and sales, variety and quality of products, profitability, labor productivity, and return on assets. Various factors may affect each index. Thus, for example, the introduction of new equipment and changes in the balance of skilled and unskilled workers have an effect on labor productivity. Enterprise profitability is determined by such factors as gross profit, the cost of plant and circulating assets, and interest on financing activities. These factors as well as the indices are objects of economic analysis. A general definition of the subject of economic analysis as it relates to a socialist enterprise is now provided: The subject of economic analysis is the productive and economic activity of the enterprise examined in close interconnection with technology and the organization of production.

The primary goal of economic analysis in Soviet enterprises is the study of the enterprise's results and its resources available for future improvement of performance. The methodology of analysis includes use of available analytical devices in combination with the technical methods of analysis. Enterprise economic analysis requires completion of an aggregate of specific activities of which the following should be noted: performing an objective review of the course and results of achievement of enterprise plans; determining additional means for plan achievement or causes of divergence from plan goals; determining effectiveness of the use of plant and circulating assets; determining causes of changes in labor productivity and studying the relationships between labor productivity and salary payments; studying the effectiveness of material incentives in reducing production expenditures and increasing labor productivity; and reviewing payment relationships with the state, the use of bank financing, and the course and results of competition stimulated by the government.

The goal of economic analysis may be successfully achieved only when the following objectives are met:

1. Analysis must be based on factual data that characterize the enterprise. The results of analysis should be compared not only with predetermined indices but also with realistic levels of accomplishment. This means that analysis should be well grounded and objective, free from the subjective impressions of the analyst.

2. Analysis should not be limited to a description of the results obtained, but should provide recommendations for specific measures to improve the enterprise's work and guidance for introduction of these measures.

3. In the course of analysis, economic indices should be examined in close connection with technological change and the use of technical methods within the production process. Analysis should bear a technical-economic character.

4. Technical-economic indices should not be studied in isolation but with recognition of their interrelationship to and dependence on one another.

5. The conclusion of analysis should always emphasize the synthesis of all enterprise resources with their redirection toward fulfillment of future operational plans.

THE METHODOLOGY OF ECONOMIC ANALYSIS

The methodology of economic analysis provides procedures and devices for developing and presenting information about economic phenomena occurring in Soviet industrial enterprises. Economic analysis in the Soviet Union is based on the Marxist principle of dialectical materialism. This means that concrete phenomena are examined as they develop, taking into consideration quantitative and qualitative changes, discovering causes and effects, and examining the whole and interconnection of all component parts. In the process of economic analysis, the causal connection and the interdependence of phenomena are discovered and studied. To accomplish this, one uses not only analysis (the breaking up of indices into parts) and synthesis (the generalization of particular data), but also such procedures as deduction (logical reasoning from the general to the particular) and induction (logical reasoning from the particular to the general). Deduction is inseparably connected to induction in economic analysis. Analysis, synthesis, induction, and deduction as methodological procedures are applied in other sciences as well. But for economic analysis the basic methodological procedures are comparison, chain substitution, and balance generalization.

Comparison is an important and widely used procedure; it is the starting point for analysis. Comparison is most often conducted in several directions by first comparing actual reported indices with corresponding predetermined indices and determining divergences from planned goals. First, the data of technical-industrial-financial plans are placed beside the actual data presented in enterprise accounting reports. Second, reported indices are compared with corresponding indices of the preceding or several preceding periods (trend-percentage analysis). Third, the efforts of an enterprise and its subdivisions (departments, shops, work teams) are compared with that of other enterprises and their subdivisions. This comparison promotes sharing of experience among many enterprises and their subdivisions. The necessary condition for use of comparative procedures is the comparability of the indices of productive economic activity being evaluated; indices must be uniform. Thus, statements must be for equivalent periods and the economic content of indices must be homogeneous.

Chain substitution or factor (variance) analysis is used widely in Soviet economic analysis when several factors simultaneously affect the phenomenon being studied. The factors may be functionally dependent on one another, often in direct or inverse proportion to one another. Using chain substitution the influence of individual factors is excluded in a prearranged manner by successive replacement of relevant factors. Thus, the effect of each factor in a complex economic operation may be calculated by substituting its actual value, often different from its planned value, into an equation in which the other factors are held constant (that is, their planned values are used). When using chain substitution the correct order of measurement of the influence of each factor must to be established. As an illustration assume that an enterprise's product cost is influenced simultaneously by deviations from norms for usage and price of materials. The difference between the enterprise's actual and planned cost of expended materials thus reflects differences from norms for both usage and price. To find the difference between the amount of materials expected to be consumed and the amount actually consumed, it is assumed that materials are expended at standard cost; the influence of price changes is excluded. Then, the quantity of materials actually expended is multiplied by the deviation from standard cost; the influence of usage is excluded. Assume the following for a specific item of material: A quantity standard of 100 tons combined with a price standard of 50 rubles per ton provides a total standard (planned) cost of 5,000 rubles; the actual quantity used of 104 tons combined with the actual price of 49 rubles provides the actual cost of 5,096 rubles. An unfavorable variance of 96 rubles (5,096 − 5,000) has resulted. The cost of materials to the enterprise has thus increased by 96 rubles, influenced by deviations from planned norms for usage and price. The cost of the product manufactured from the material is higher by 200 rubles as a result of the difference between planned and actual usage (100 tons − 104 tons × 50 rubles). The cost of the product is lower by 104 rubles as a result of the difference between standard cost and actual price (50 rubles − 49 rubles × 104 tons). Thus, as a result of a 200-ruble overexpenditure of material, and a simultaneous 104-ruble saving from the reduction in price, the overall cost of production has increased by 96 rubles (200 − 104).

In the process of analysis it is necessary to determine rational relationships between resources and the efficiency of their use and between assets and the sources of their formation. Comparison for study of items such as use of workers' and machine time and working capital is carried out using the methodological procedure of balance generalization, the procedure of breaking a whole into component parts (time available into hours worked and idle time). The methodology of economic analysis provides for use of a number of methodological devices from other sciences. The most important are presentation in graphs, composition of analytical tables, subdivision and grouping, and mathematical-statistical techniques. Presentation in graphs is useful for analysis of the composition and interrelationship of economic phenomena. Analytical tables composed from planned and actual enterprise data have the same purpose. Graphs and diagrams are often used to illustrate analytical tables. The rhythm of product output, for example, can be illustrated by a graph in which one line (perforated) indicates the planned output of product by time periods (working days) and a second line (solid) indicates the actual output of product for the same periods, thereby revealing deviations from planned output. The use of this device in enterprise shops and departments provides continuing visual information about the process of plan fulfillment and encourages the timely adoption of measures for achieving rhythmical output of production.

Subdivision and grouping of economic indicators create the basis for a deeper and broader evaluation of enterprise performance. Complex expenditures, such as the cost of a unit of product, are studied more thoroughly by subdividing their values by economic composition into homogeneous groups and subgroups. Individual economic processes, such as sales of products, are subjected to economic grouping to obtain combined indices. Grouping allows determination of causal relationships and interdependence among processes and the separation of the essential in economic processes from the accidental. Economic grouping is especially important in the analysis of the combined information of many enterprises.

Mathematical-statistical techniques play an important role in economic analysis. Their use is necessary for analysis of the quantitative aspects of economic phenomena and for a more precise understanding of their qualitative aspects. Almost all forms of elementary and higher mathematics, especially statistics and linear programming, are useful. When there is no strict functional dependence between phenomena but rather a plural and correlational dependence, the relationship of phenomena to each other is studied using statistical methods. In these situations, one can determine the degree to which many factors operating at one time influence the index being studied; the closeness of the interrelationship among factors may be established. Analysis using correlation makes it possible to determine how the volume of product output, the type of production, and other factors affect complex costs. The calculation of average values is necessary for analysis of the level of labor productivity and the cost of products. Linear programming is used for prediction of economic activity and for determination of optimal planning goals. In an industrial enterprise, the optimal load of equipment, the rational dispensing of materials, and the ideal volume of output from a production line may be determined using this technique. If equations for solution of a mathematical problem are not linear, the economic phenomena can be analyzed using nonlinear methods of mathematical programming.

DEVELOPMENT AND USE OF ECONOMIC INFORMATION

Economic analysis is based on a wide and varied range of information relating to the activity of an enterprise. Economic information includes that characterizing the economic aspects of the enterprise's productive and financial activity. Economic indices are the units of measure of economic information. Economic information is utilized in the management of individual enterprises, groups of related enterprises, and the national economy. According to its use within the management process economic information is classified as planning, operational, accounting, and statistical.

Economic analysis rests primarily on accounting data rather than on purely operational or statistical reports because it is in enterprise accounting departments that economic resources and processes are most fully, systematically, and continuously recorded. Actual accounting data are essential for objective evaluation of achievement of the operational plan, discovery of untapped resources, and insuring the safety of state property. Actual data are compared with indices in planning guidelines received by the enterprise from the government and also with indices in goals established independently by the enterprise. Statistical reports are used in the evaluation of plan fulfillment and they are often based on accounting data. Data from technical documentation characterizes the status of the enterprise's equipment, the enterprise's overall level of technology, and its organization for production; they are used in carrying out economic analysis as a supplement to financially oriented reports. Information on norms presented in ministry reference manuals, instructions, and price lists is frequently used in analysis. Nevertheless, the financial information developed cannot totally reflect the results of enterprise activity and its financial condition since some accounting data are at times incomplete and many aspects of the enterprise's work do not lend themselves to systematic accounting. Therefore information from other sources is useful and necessary.

Nonaccounting information frequently used in economic analysis includes data from enterprise minutes, decisions of industrial conferences, and reports from inspections of enterprise shops and departments by Communist Party representatives and officials of trade union organizations. Source documents and operational summaries are required to carry out operational analysis in individual parts of the enterprise (departments, shops, work places) for specific time periods. This immediate analysis enables the enterprise to uncover problems and deficiencies promptly and to strengthen measures found effective. Operational analysis, however, emphasizes individual economic operations within the enterprise and not the productive and economic activity of the enterprise as a whole. Much importance is attached to systematic analysis of enterprise economic activity for established periods on the basis of interim and annual statements, but these statements reflect only the fundamental monetary indices of economic activity. It is necessary to supplement the basic financial statements with additional disclosures and appendices containing operational and statistical information.

Personnel from enterprise accounting departments and other specialized departments conduct economic analysis of all enterprise productive and economic activity. In the accounting department, preliminary control of economic operations and use and conservation of enterprise resources is combined with control later achieved through systematic analysis. In addition to its own responsibilities and activities, enterprise accounting departments provide assistance to government and Communist Party analysts. The enterprise financial department monitors the enterprise's financial condition and fulfillment of its overall financial plan. The economics laboratory develops the methodology for planning, accounting, and economic analysis used in the enterprise. The chief economist is responsible for conducting a thorough economic analysis of the productive and economic activity of the enterprise; he is in charge of the organization and coordination of this activity. The planning department develops the analytical basis for enterprise operational goals according to centrally planned guidelines. It analyzes the output indices for each shop, department, and the total enterprise but, most important, it analyzes indices for production cost. The department also analyzes the effects of organizational and technological changes that have been implemented.

The supplies (provisioning) department reviews on a daily basis the observance of stock levels for production materials, fuel, and spare parts. The supplies department also monitors consumption of materials by production departments and information on payments to suppliers. The sales department analyzes the delivery of products to customers, the flow of customer payments, and correspondence of actual inventories of finished products with amounts established by norms. The labor and salary department exercises systematic control over the salary fund; it analyzes labor productivity and studies the effectiveness of compensation and incentive systems. The scientific analysis department studies work processes in all divisions of the enterprise, analyzes the effectiveness of organizational and technical operations, and determines appropriate standards for measurement of equipment use and work time. It works with the labor and salary department to evaluate and improve the system of labor organization within the enterprise. The technical control department provides a technical analysis of the quality of products. It estimates the effects of changes in product quality and composition on production costs. It also works with other departments to establish the causes of substandard production and those responsible.

The enterprise chief technologist and his staff monitor the technical aspects of the production process, such as observance of formulas for mixing raw materials. In cooperation with other departments, the chief technologist analyzes the effectiveness of new materials, equipment, and processes. The chief mechanic investigates causes for idling of equipment and determines those responsible. His office determines the most efficient way to repair equipment, analyzes the accuracy of repair cost estimates, and determines the effectiveness of equipment modernization. The chief energy specialist monitors the observance of norms for production and consumption of all kinds of energy within the enterprise and reviews the consumption and cost of purchased energy.

SPECIFIC ANALYSIS OF ENTERPRISE OPERATIONAL PLANS

Economic analysis of enterprise technical-industrial-financial plans is usually performed in the following order: analysis of plans for product output and related cost; analysis of plans for distribution, sales, and profitability; and analysis of the financial condition of the enterprise. For each section of the general program of analysis, the work is conducted in the following stages: general evaluation of the fulfillment of the plan, discovery and measurement of underlying factors, and determination of interrelationships and their parallel or successive influence on results.

Analysis of achievement of the production program includes analysis of the volume of commodity production, determination of the effect of incomplete production on commodity output, analysis of fulfillment of requirements for variety and quantities of products, analysis of the production cycle, and analysis of related plans affecting achievement of the production program (plans for labor and salaries, materials and supplies, and construction, acquisition, and use of plant assets). Analysis of product cost is accomplished within the reviews previously mentioned. Also reviewed is the determination of unit costs, the calculation and disposition of variances, and expenditures per ruble of sales revenue for commodity products. Also subject to analysis are costs related to fuel and energy consumption, maintenance and use of equipment, manufacturing overhead, and spoilage. Analysis of plan fulfillment for product distribution and sales and enterprise profitability includes review of relevant economic indicators and the use of funds for economic stimulation and special purposes. The analysis of financial condition considers enterprise use of allotted resources and bank credit, the use and reserves of circulating assets, enterprise liability payment discipline, and concludes with a general review of enterprise solvency. The process of economic analysis is now complete: Conclusions are drawn from the results; summaries are prepared and deficiencies and their causes are documented; responsibility is determined and penalties assigned; and proposals to eliminate deficiencies and solidify gains are developed.

Appendix A

Extracts from the Criminal Code of the Russian Soviet Federated Socialist Republic

Sabotage (Article 69). Commission or omission of action with intent to undermine industry, transport, agriculture, the monetary system, trade, or any branch of the national economy or activity of a social organization. A strike will be classified as a crime under this article.

Penalty: Imprisonment from eight to fifteen years with confiscation of property and subsequent exile for a period of two to five years.

Smuggling (Article 78). Illegal transport of goods or other valuables across the state border of the USSR.

Penalty: Imprisonment from three to ten years with confiscation of property and subsequent exile for a period of two to five years.

Violation of rules governing currency transactions (Article 88). Speculation of currency in valuables or currency in paper money.

Penalty: Imprisonment from three to fifteen years with confiscation of property and subsequent exile for a period of two to five years. Violations with aggravating circumstances are punishable by execution with confiscation of property.

Theft of state or society's property (Articles 89, 90, 91). These articles classify theft according to method and scale: theft by stealing, theft by robbery, theft by plundering, theft by abuse of office, theft by swindling, and theft on a large scale.

Penalty: Imprisonment from one to fifteen years with confiscation of property. Large-scale theft is punishable by execution with confiscation of property.

Issuing poor quality products (Article 152). Issuing from an industrial enterprise products of poor quality or production which does not meet state standards.

Penalty: Imprisonment up to three years.

Overstatement and other distortions of accounting records and statements (Article 152.1).

Penalty: Imprisonment up to three years.

Deception of customers (Article 156). Cheating in measurements or weights, increasing prices, miscalculation of price, and other consumer fraud.

Penalty: Imprisonment up to seven years with confiscation of property.

Abuse of authority or office (Article 171). Deliberate use of position or office for personal gain.

Penalty: Imprisonment up to eight years.

Negligence (Article 172). Failure to perform duties or improper performance of duties by an official.

Penalty: Imprisonment up to three years.

Appendix B

Schema of General Ledger
Account Correspondence

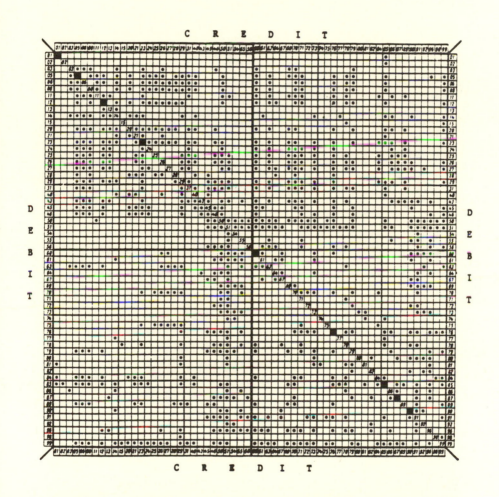

Source: E. T. Astashkevicher [E. Ash], <u>Accounting for a Machine-Building Plant</u> (Moscow: Mashinostroenie, 1979), 82-83.

[a]A black dot at the point of intersection of debit and credit rows indicates that a correspondence of the two accounts is permissible. A black square at the intersection indicates that correspondence between subsidiary accounts within controlling accounts is permissible. If the space of intersection is blank the accounts indicated cannot correspond under any circumstances.

Appendix C

Chart of Accounts to be Used by All Soviet Industrial and Construction Enterprises

I.   Plant Assets
    01.   Plant Assets
    02.   Accumulated Depreciation
    03.   Capital Repairs

II. Inventories
    05.   Production Materials
    06.   Fuel and Combustible Materials
    07.   Construction Materials and Equipment for Installation
    08.   Spare Parts for Plant Assets
    09.   Younger Animals and Animals on Fattening
    12.   Low-cost Expendable Items
    13.   Depletion of Low-cost Expendable Items
    14.   Reappraisal of Nonplant Assets
    15.   Acquisition of Nonplant Assets
    16.   Transportation and Acquisition Expenses

III. Manufacturing Costs
    20.   Principal Work in Process
    21.   Self-manufactured Semifinished Products
    23.   Auxiliary Department
    24.   Expenses for Use an Maintenance of Equipment
    25.   Departmental Manufacturing Overhead
    26.   Factory Manufacturing Overhead
    28.   Cost of Spoiled Production

Source: Ministry of Finance of the USSR, Chart of Accounts and Instructions for its Use, 1985, 4-9.

VIII. Funds and Reserves

      85.   State Equity Fund
      86.   Amortization Fund
      87.   Funds for Economic Stimulation
      88.   Funds for Special Purposes
      89.   Reserves for Future Expenses and Payments

IX. Bank Loans and Financing
      90.   Short-term Bank Loans Payable
      92.   Long-term Bank Loans Payable
      93.   Financing for Capital Investments
      94.   Financing for Creating a Principal Herd of Animals
      96.   Special Purpose Financing/Revenue from Special Sources

Off-Balance-Sheet Accounts
      001.   Plant Assets on Lease
      002.   Merchandise and Goods in Custody
      003.   Equipment Accepted for Installation
      004.   Blank Forms Under Strict Security
      005.   Losses from Uncollectible Accounts Receivable

Notes

CHAPTER 1

1. Central Statistical Administration, *National Economy of the USSR for 1988* (Moscow: Finance and Statistics, 1989), 19.

2. Alexander Zinoviev, *V Predverii Raia* (In anticipation of paradise) (Lausanne: L'Age D'Homme, 1979), 23-24.

3. Mark Popovsky, "Six Portraits of One Face," *Novoye Russkoye Slovo*, 2 June 1989, 3.

CHAPTER 2

1. Vladimir Ilyich Lenin, *Polnoe Sobranie Sochinenii,* 55 vols., vol. 36, (Full collection of works) (Moscow: Gosudarstvennoye Izdatel'stvo Politicheskoy Literatury, 1962), 300.

2. Ibid. 37: 21-22.

3. Ibid. 33: 101.

4. *Criminal Code of the Russian Soviet Federated Socialist Republic*, 1971, Articles 209 and 209.1.

CHAPTER 3

1. Statistical data describing each branch of the Soviet economy for 1988 within Chapter 3 have been derived by adjustment of data from the Central Statistical Administration, *National Economy of the USSR for 1987* (Moscow: Finance and Statistics, 1988).

2. It is estimated that 30 to 50 percent of dairy products, 30 to 40 percent of meat products, more than half of all fruit and vegetables, and almost three-fourths of all potatoes are produced on the 3 percent of Soviet land that is privately used.

3. In many of the large cities various systems are used to limit consumption of specific food products; tokens may be issued to limit consumption of butter to 400 grams a month per person. Side by side with these systems are closed outlets which are used by the Soviet elite to purchase food and other items at very low prices.

4. The average Soviet industrial and officer worker, earning less than one ruble per hour, must work 4 hours to earn enough for 2.2 pounds of bologna.

CHAPTER 4

1. All Soviet products are appraised by quality before distribution; they are then marked and priced accordingly.

2. Contribution margin is the excess of enterprise revenues over its variable (changing) costs; the tendency of income is the ratio of enterprise income to the average cost of its assets.

CHAPTER 5

1. Central Statistical Administration, *National Economy of the USSR for 1988* (Moscow: Finance and Statistics, 1989), 624-28.

2. Enterprises are the primary recipients of credit; loans are seldom granted to individuals, usually only for construction of a home or purchase of furniture.

3. Government officials, businesspeople, and tourists travelling to or from the United States may exchange dollars and rubles at the established official rate or pursue black market conversion; it is expected that the ruble will become fully convertible during 1991 or 1992.

CHAPTER 6

1. Roman Redlikh, *Soviet Society* (Frankfort-on-Main, Germany: Posev, 1972), 83-84.

2. Anticipated revisions prompted by *perestroika* are expected to legalize certain economic activities now considered criminal.

CHAPTER 7

1. Rose Brady, "Help Wanted, and Fast," *Business Week*, 15 June 1990, 128-30.
2. Increasing worker dissatisfaction, decreasing product quality, lack of ethics in management, etc.

CHAPTER 8

1. Analytical or subsidiary accounts are subaccounts with common characteristics (customers, inventory items, etc.) maintained in a separate subsidiary ledger for purposes of control and convenience; a synthetic or controlling account is maintained in the general or principal ledger to summarize amounts in each group of analytical accounts.

CHAPTER 10

1. As the economic reforms resulting from perestroika take effect, the content of the Soviet balance sheet, and the accounts included in the single chart of accounts for Soviet industrial enterprises will reflect any changes from state ownership to private ownership and new forms of organization such as joint ventures with Western businesses.
2. The existence of a single chart of accounts does not exclude the use of special accounts and techniques to meet the individual requirements of special activities and organizations such as those under the Ministry of Foreign Trade.

CHAPTER 12

1. Some industrial enterprises raise animals and farm products for distribution to workers.

CHAPTER 15

1. Specific cost accounting procedures are also applicable within the following divisions of the machine-building industry: heavy equipment; chemical and oil machine-building; and lathe, press, and light machinery building.

CHAPTER 19

1. The government permits enterprises to include certain expenditures for repairs and capital construction as equivalent to commodity production to stimulate these activities within the enterprise.

Bibliography

Ash, Ehiel. "Soviet Style of Teaching Accounting." *Journal of Accounting Education* 3 (Spring 1985): 37-46.

Astashkevicher, E. T. [Ehiel Ash]. *Accounting for a Machine-Building Plant*. Moscow: Mashinostroenie, 1970.

Astashkevicher, E. T. [Ehiel Ash]. *Economic Analysis of Machine-Building Plant Activity*. Moscow: Mashinostroenie, 1971.

Bezrukih, P. C., ed. *Accounting*. Moscow: Finance and Statistics, 1982.

Brady, Rose. "Help Wanted, and Fast." *Business Week* (June 15, 1990): 128-30.

Central Statistical Administration of the USSR. *National Economy of the USSR for 1987*. Moscow: Finance and Statistics, 1988.

Central Statistical Administration of the USSR. *National Economy of the USSR for 1988*. Moscow: Finance and Statistics, 1989.

Chastain, C. E. "Soviet Accounting Lags Behind the Needs of Enterprise Managers." *Management International Review* 22, no. 4 (1982): 12-18.

Criminal Code of the Russian Soviet Federated Socialist Republic.

Lenin, Vladimir Ilyich *Polnoe Sobranie Sochinenii* (Full collection of works). 55 vols. Moscow: Gosudarstvennoye Isdatel'stvo Politicheskoy Literatury, 1962.

Ministry of Finance of the USSR. *Chart of Accounts and Instructions for its Use*. Approval no. 40, 1985.

Redlikh, Roman. *Soviet Society*. Frankfort-on-Main, Germany: Posev, 1972.

"Six Portraits of One Face." *Novoye Rosskoye Slovo* [Russian daily newspaper] (June 2, 1989).

Verbov, G. D. and N. I. Pervuhin. *Manual of Normative Documents on Accounting*. 3 vols. Moscow: Finansy, 1980.

Zinoviev, Alexander. *V Predverii Raia* (In anticipation of paradise). Lausanne: L'Age D'Homme, 1979.

Index

ABOUT THE AUTHORS

EHIEL ASH is Associate Professor of Accounting at Iona College in New Rochelle, New York. He is the author of many books and articles on Soviet accounting and the analysis of financial statements and reports.

ROBERT STRITTMATTER is Associate Professor of Accounting at Iona College. He also has recently developed and published accounting computer software for educational use.